SEX AND MORALITY
Who Is Teaching Our Sex Standards?

SEX AND MORALITY

Who Is Teaching
Our Sex Standards?

Dr. Ruth Westheimer
Dr. Louis Lieberman

HARCOURT BRACE JOVANOVICH, PUBLISHERS

Boston San Diego New York

Requests for permission to make copies of any part of the work
should be mailed to:
Permissions, Harcourt Brace Jovanovich, Publishers,
Orlando, Florida 32887.

Designed by Iris Kramer

Printed in the United States of America

Library of Congress Cataloging-in-Publication Data
Westheimer, Ruth K. (Ruth Karola). 1928–
Sex and morality: who is teaching our sex standards? / Ruth
Westheimer, Louis Lieberman. — 1st ed.
p.   cm.
Includes Index.
ISBN 0-15-181390-6
1. Sexual ethics—United States.   2. Sex—Religious aspects.
3. Choice (Psychology)   4. United States—Moral conditions.
I. Lieberman, Louis.   II. Title.
HQ32.W466   1988   88-6178
306.7—dc19   CIP

First edition
A   B   C   D   E

Receive my instruction, and not silver,
And knowledge rather than choice gold.
For wisdom is better than rubies,
And all things desirable are not to be compared unto her!

(Proverbs 8:10,11)

Contents

Acknowledgements

First, to those at Harcourt Brace Jovanovich: We cannot create the accolades you truly deserve. To find the old world charm and grace and intelligence of publishers Klaus and Alice Peters still present in this marketplace of book publishing was indeed a pleasure. Your enthusiasm and patience and advice made our tasks unusually satisfying. Undoubtedly because you are so nice, you have developed a first-rate staff who were wonderful to work with: Susan McCulley, Assistant Editor, was a dynamo of efficiency to bridge the miles between New York and Boston; Carolyn Artin, Managing Editor, and Iris Kramer and Ezra C. Holston, Production Managers, made our transition of words from computer to final print smooth and created a beautiful product.

To Eve Mendelsohn, freelance copy editor, whose perceptive comments and patient corrections of our free-flowing English make this a far more readable book than it otherwise would have been.

To Meyer Glaser and Cliff Rubin, our research assistants, who helped us through the maze of literature for our substantive areas: It was a job well done!

To Mary (Maria) Cuadrado, a special person, who gave so generously of her time, warmth, encouragement and love. But more important than her great skills in the use of computers was her personal relationship with Lou—without you, we would have had much down time in many ways. Thank you.

Writing books in subject areas related to psychology and the raising of children always raises more questions for authors than they are able to answer. We were very fortunate in being able to draw upon the vast knowledge and professional experience of such friends as Mark J. Blechner, Ph.D., David Goslin, Ph.D., and Nina Lief, M.D.

For clarification and insights into some of the complex and controversial bio-social issues touched upon in this book, we turned to a brilliant and witty scholar and researcher: John Money, Ph.D., Professor Emeritus of medical psychology and pediatrics at Johns Hopkins University. His comments about where science may still go always excited the mind and imagination.

Two more friends who have made the creation of this book a much more viable endeavor are Pierre Lehu and John A. Silberman.

Acknowledgements

To Monsignor Joseph A. Dunne, Chaplain, New York City Police Department (Ret).), for his patient help with Biblical references and his helping us to understand the spiritual basis for morality, a grateful thanks.

We owe a great debt to Rabbi Robert L. Lehman of the Hebrew Tabernacle of Washington Heights who gave us much encouragement for this project and helped us with an understanding of the complexities of modern religious thought.

Often, we hear silly anecdotes and jokes about "The Rabbi and the Priest." But the rabbi and the priest in this book are representative of the best in this noble profession. We drew upon our many years of friendship with Rabbi Leonard Kravitz and Father Finbarr Corr and called upon them for extensive interviews for this book. We were again impressed with their sensitivity, knowledge and commitment to the moral fiber of life, and we are grateful indeed.

Other religious leaders who have broadened our own understanding of the complexities of and necessity for moral commitment, from a broad spectrum of religious orientations, and whose thinking and words are found in this book, are Bishop Paul Moore, Jr., of the Episcopal Diocese of New York; Dr. James B. Nelson, professor of Christian ethics at the United Theological Seminary of the Twin Cities, in Minnesota; Dr. Robert E. Schuller of the Crystal Cathedral in Garden Grove, California; and Bishop John S. Spong of the Episcopal Diocese of Newark, New Jersey.

A special mention must be given to four unique lay religious leaders from the New York Mission of The Church of Jesus Christ of Latter-day Saints (known informally as the Mormons): Elder Madison H. Thomas, M.D., Sister Marian Peterson Thomas, Elder Boyd L. Fugal, Sister Venice Jacob Fugal. They provided special insight as to how religion and family work together to provide a consistent moral education. We are thankful for the generosity of their time and interest in our endeavors.

And finally, to those people whose assistance was of the greatest importance to the growth of this book: Alas, we cannot mention you by name. You are the many who must remain anonymous and are the soul of this book. We have learned a great deal from you, and you have touched us more by your willingness to share your intimate thoughts and feelings than we can ever fully acknowledge. Thank you.

CHAPTER 1

Sexual Choices:
Why Such Difficulties?

A middle-aged man thinks to himself: "I don't know what's wrong with our sex life, I don't seem to have the same urge for Marge as before. Maybe if I had sex with that new girl in purchasing who's always flirting with me, I wouldn't feel so much strain at home."

A young mother catches her 7-year-old-daughter in the nude with a 6-year-old boy examining each other's genitals. She reacts with a great feeling of anxiety and thinks: "My God, she is only a baby, and she is already doing something wrong. She must be punished for such dirty sex acts."

A 16-year-old boy and girl are lovers. One day, she finds out that she is pregnant. They discuss their options: Marriage, abortion, or giving the baby up for adoption seem most likely. How do they decide?

A young woman in her late teens wants to keep her boyfriend. Her mother keeps telling her that sex before marriage is wrong, but she thinks: "How could something that everybody is doing be so wrong? And besides, what's so important about a hymen anyway?"

A teenager whose family has just purchased a hot tub for the basement invites friends of both sexes over for a party.

After a while they all tell her that they would like to go skinny-dipping together in the tub. She was brought up to believe that nudity in front of strangers is not only immodest but immoral. What should she do?

How do we know what choices to make in situations such as these? How do we know what is right and what is wrong? Moral and and immoral? Unfortunately, we don't always know what is "right," and more unfortunately, the "wrong" choice can sometimes have long-lasting and tragic repercussions. It is out of a growing concern for the consequences of such moral choices that this book was conceived.

As we reflect back on how we came to write this book, it appears to us that it was almost inevitable that this collaboration was undertaken. For some readers who are familiar with the books and articles each of us has written, the subject matter of this book—the communication of sexual morals, attitudes and values—may seem a large departure from both the focus of most of our previous publications—human sexual behavior for one of us and substance abuse for the other—as well as from our usual respective styles of writing. This is really not so because one cannot talk seriously about sexual behavior or drug use behavior without the subject of values and morals being not only in the back of one's mind but also, many times, the direct topic of discussion. The writing style will be a little different from that of our previous works. This is necessitated in part by the subject matter as well as by our objective: to reach as wide an audience as possible that we believe needs and wants to have issues of sexual values discussed without the philosophic and social science terminology or complicated conceptual frameworks and theories that so often accompany such discussions. On the other hand, we will try not to trivialize so important a subject as moral decision making by pretending that there are always simple and clear answers to one's questions.

This book reflects much of the experiences and thoughts we have had for a large part of our adult lives—each of us filling

2

the roles of parent, educator and therapist. Our approach is also an outgrowth of our respective backgrounds. These were quite different backgrounds, but with important similarities that bear on some of the thoughts expressed in this book— backgrounds in which choices based upon certain values and value systems made all the difference. Ruth Westheimer's background had its roots in the nightmare of history that culminated in World War II, leaving an orphaned girl who had to build a new life with the uncertainties of bewildering choices and European values that by then seemed to have failed. Lou Lieberman's background during the same years— growing up in poverty and violence in the slums of Brownsville in Brooklyn, New York—also pivoted on choices. Wrong choices meant no escape from poverty or worse, but his family's traditional European values, which were the source of strength to make correct decisions, were mocked in public schools as not being "American" enough.

We have both thought a good deal about the significance of values and their relationship to choices that have consequences ranging from joy to much suffering. We have thought about this both from a personal point of view and as part of the rigorous sociological and philosophic educational experience in that unique New School for Social Research in New York City, where we met as graduate students nearly thirty years ago. Most of the original members of the Graduate Faculty of Political and Social Science (the "Faculty in Exile") were great European scholars who were rescued from impending destruction during the Nazi era. Our professors knew from firsthand experience that wrong choices, emerging in part from confused values and corrupted moral codes, could be devastating not only to individuals but to great and civilized nations as well.

Although our careers have developed along somewhat different lines since those days, our professional activities and work as educators and members of the healing profession has brought us into contact with many people who were and are in great emotional pain and social difficulty, often because of

3

wrong choices they have made in life. We have often talked with each other and with our friends and colleagues about this very important problem of why so many people of all ages seem to lack the foresight, ability, common sense or whatever to make the right choices about everyday but crucial matters such as choosing friends, keeping up with school, going out with appropriate people of the opposite sex and avoiding unwanted pregnancies. We have heard our colleagues and others blame it on the "me" generation attitudes of the 1960s and 1970s, but we know that many people were making the wrong choices long before then. It appears to us that much of the criticism directed at young people is based on the assumption that they "know better" but for some other reason choose to do the wrong thing. This assumption has bothered us, particularly in the area of sexual choices, because we aren't sure that these young men and women always do "know better" and can really make the correct choices.

It was and still is our view, undoubtedly reinforced by our backgrounds, that moral choices should not be made *ad hominem*; that is, depending on the person or emotions. Moral and ethical choices depend on some kind of system or moral code to provide the guidelines for people to use in these new situations. Do these young people really have a moral code that they understand and accept to help them make correct decisions, or is that code merely in the minds, prayers and hopes of their parents? How can people learn to make these choices as unique, individual personalities, particularly as young persons without sufficient experience to reflect on previous choices? We cannot be born with the wisdom of Solomon. Young or old, we cannot spend our lives in the analytic study of ethical and moral systems and logic and the probability of outcomes. We need a clear voice in the back of our minds reminding us that there is a sound basis for the correct decisions we must make—not one based upon impulse, passion, drink, fear of rejection or whatever.

Most people assume that everyone gets and knows a moral

4

code but chooses to reject it. We frequently hear from politicians and religious leaders that as a civilized nation of laws and rules we must believe in the "traditional values"; that there are basic "moral truths" that we should accept. The problem is that they rarely explain what they mean by "traditional values" or "moral truths." Furthermore, these truths or guidelines are sometimes different for different religious and ethnic groups. Even though adults may urge their children and even each other to accept "traditional" values, they may have different ideas about what these values are. How can parents be sure that their children understand their particular notion of values and morality? Even if the children do understand, do these values make sense to them on a day-to-day basis?

Have we, as a society, deluded ourselves into thinking that at least one (or even better, that all three) of our main social institutions responsible for teaching moral codes—the family, religion and education—have done their job and transmitted these moral norms for decision making adequately to each succeeding generation? We will raise this complicated question at different places in this book and try to answer it as best as we can. Current confusions in different parts of our society and on the part of many people, both young and old, raise serious questions about the effectiveness of our moral educations. It is true that people are different when it comes to various aspects of moral decision making, but they are alike in the sense that all humans need guidelines, particularly in the years during which we develop what we end up believing is our own *personal* value system. Without values consistent with our accepted moral beliefs, our choices may be confused and our responsibility for the consequences questionable.

We believe that a firm sense of traditional concepts of right and wrong, the difference between moral and immoral behavior and a responsibility for the consequences of choices is fundamental to a civilized society. But how are these understood by different people in practical, everyday terms? We know that the Old and the New Testaments are the bases of our values

5

and moral codes, but what about the different interpretations and emphases in different religions and denominations?

We cannot take the position in this book that one religion's moral and ethical standards are better than another religion's or even better than a secular, humanist moral code. That would be foolish in a pluralistic society such as we have in the United States. In a free society, all adults may follow any religious affiliation of their choice or choose not to have one at all. But this is not the same as saying that we should be free *not* to have a set of moral principles to guide us; such freedom would not be desirable in a civilized nation. We need values to help us make daily choices in life, and we have to learn these values from our families or get them from somewhere else. The nature of these values and how we acquire them is what we are going to explore in this book.

Why should this be so much of a problem? Why can't we do just like our parents did? Because, we believe, no society in the history of humankind has provided a milieu in which people grow up with as many alternatives for social behavior as we find in the societies of Western culture today, and in the United States in particular. Why is this so? Because freedom of choice and variations in social behavior depend upon the awareness of available alternatives. In other words, if you believe that you may only choose between job A or job B because you think that you are not eligible for any other positions, you will pick only A or B or nothing at all. But on the other hand, if you know that there are people with the same background and brains as you who are also able get jobs C to Z, any one of those job choices can become an option for you. Deciding which job would be best for you requires a different approach to the problem than merely gaining access to information about alternative opportunities. When it comes to the area of choosing the "right" sexual behavior, it is important for us to realize as educators, parents and others who have to deal with the consequences of these choices that young persons, like their

6

elders, face a bewildering array of choices for human social behavior.

A parallel from the drug use area: We may not like the presence of heroin or cocaine in our society today, but we must be aware that for now we are free to choose to use these drugs or not. Furthermore, because we are also free to be oblivious to the consequences if we so choose, we may make the wrong and destructive choice. Are there clear and unequivocal guidelines to help us, particularly younger persons, to make the correct choice? Unfortunately, there aren't any, which has forced some well intentioned people to engage in campaigns such as "Just Say No to Drugs." We think this approach is insulting to the intelligence of young persons since it implies a basis for the decision making that denies them the ability to make choices. It says, in effect, "Just say no because *we* tell you to."

It is equally ineffectual to tell a young person to remain a virgin until marriage because *we*, as parents, want her (or him) to. There must be a clear moral code that both parent and child *accept* and that includes virginity as only one element. This moral code should then serve as a sound and meaningful basis for choosing to remain a virgin. We are also free to choose whether or not to use contraceptives in acts of sexual intimacy, and here too, as with drug use, we may also choose to be oblivious to the consequences of not using contraceptives. But, just as we cannot ignore the consequences of addiction when it occurs, we cannot ignore the consequences of teenage pregnancy. The choice of having sex, whether or not to use contraceptives, sex outside of and before marriage, are all moral questions that should be held up to a consistent and acceptable moral code learned from childhood on.

Why do we have so many alternative behaviors to choose from? For one thing, we are among the best educated peoples in the world. Young persons are not only aware of the behaviors of their own ethnic and religious groups but also of the ways and beliefs of others. Although some groups choose not to expose their children to the values, belief systems and lifestyles of people who are different, most Americans seem to have come to the position that it is good and valuable for people to see and learn about how different groups vary, about their different foods and languages, their customs and religious expressions.

We also have more television sets per capita than any nation. We communicate to each other on a global basis. It would be very hard to deny that television has an immense impact on learning and conveys an awareness of the vast range of human behavior to its viewers. This we believe has a liberalizing and educational impact far greater than that of the printed page.

People travel a lot, not only in this country but to our neighbors on northern and southern borders as well as to Europe, Asia, the Middle East and elsewhere. It is difficult to travel and experience other cultures both within our borders and elsewhere and still maintain the ethnocentric point of view that *our* own ethnic group has the best music, the best food, the best clothing and, also, the best or only religion and values worth considering.

Finally, during the past century, the migrations to the cities— to the metropolis and the megalopolis—have resulted in social environments that are less controlling and less supervised, with the consequent weakening of ties to parental value systems. This is much different from the world of our parents, grand-parents and great-grandparents who lived in smaller communities where it was easier to reinforce the same values of everyone else in the community and easier to pass these values on to children.

Another factor in our decision to write this book at this particular time stems from our concerns about the terrible waste of lives from AIDS, the acquired immune deficiency syndrome. As of the time we write this book, the fall of 1987, no solution to this dreadful disease appears imminent. We, along with our many colleagues in the area of human sexuality,

8

do not believe in the concept of "safe sex." At the same time, we are not so naive as to think that the solution to this problem lies in the well-meaning but unrealistic approach of the "say no to sex" advocates. Both young people and old have had sex before, during and outside of marriage since marriage first appeared as a social institution. Whether one says that sex outside of marriage is immoral or sinful or leads to venereal disease has not stopped the passionate and spontaneous expression of sexual desires in the past and probably will not in the future. However, this does not mean that there is no value in public and private discussions of the morality and ethics of such behavior; the more awareness everyone has of the issues involved—the health, the emotional, the familial, the responsibilities and the moral—the more likely people are to make responsible choices. We hope that discussions around the issues in this book, many of which are directly or indirectly related to the possibility of the transmission of sexual diseases, will prove a valuable tool for persons on different sides of these issues.

All this brings us to how the book will be organized. At the beginning of each chapter dealing with specific sexual practices, we present a brief history of the origins of some of the sexual norms insofar as scholars have knowledge of them. We proceed then by presenting the issues as we see them. We have asked a number of outstanding representatives from different religions for their views on what they would like to see communicated to the adherents of their religion when it comes to issues related to sexual behavior—their religion's perspectives on which behaviors are permitted or forbidden, which are sins, which are morally wrong in specific situations, etc. At times, this may prove to be a difficult task because these views are in a state of flux in many segments of the religious community. Thus, the traditional viewpoint may have to be presented even though church leaders are still trying to clarify the issues. Because some of the moral positions are so theologically complicated, people who belong to a church or synagogue

9

often have only a vague notion of where their religion stands on many of these issues. The objective of these discussions with religious leaders is not to provide a comprehensive or definitive work on sexual moral codes but to begin to develop a framework for discussion so that we can see the relationship between different aspects of sexual morality for different religions.

Once we have done this, we present the results of our discussions with ordinary people who have had to make decisions in these matters at some point in their lives. We will try to present as fairly as possible what they think the position of their religion is, how they learned their moral codes in sexual matters, what influenced them in one way or another and what they will teach their children. We will explore with them why some moral messages seem more acceptable for some people than for others. Why do some sexual standards and norms (rules) serve as guidelines and "brakes" so that they help people conform to the traditional expectations of their religious groups while other sexual norms do not? Are some ways in which moral norms are transmitted from one generation to another more effective than others? Why are only some young adults willing to accept these traditional moral norms as they are currently presented? Does television or radio or sex education courses or exposure to the liberal education of college play any role in the rejection of traditional sex and marital norms? Are the moral norms accepted in principle but rejected in practice? We also present, in the words of the people we have talked with, their perception of what might have gone wrong in the transmission of these norms, thus persuading them to behave in a contrary manner.

As probably noted from the table of contents, we do not cover many sexual behaviors that may be of concern to some people. We do not discuss such sexual behaviors as sadomasochism (inflicting or receiving pain with pleasure), bondage and discipline (tying up a voluntary partner or engaging in deliberate master-slave relationships), pedophilia (sexual acts with children), exhibitionism (revealing sex organs in public to

10

an unwilling audience), voyeurism (looking at others engaging in sex or in the nude against their wishes) or other behaviors that many professionals call deviant sexual acts. The reason for omitting these is that they are so often related to emotional problems and may involve elements of compulsive behavior that are more suitable for a clinical study of deviant sexual practices. We are more concerned with the morality issues in "acceptable" sex, that is, behaviors that clinical psychologists and psychiatrists do not generally consider indicative of an emotionally disturbed individual. In one sense, it reflects a bias as to what we think is sexually acceptable to most persons in our society.

It is our sincere hope that this book will lead to new and better methods of communicating issues concerning sexual and marital moral behavior and norms as well as guidelines for moral decision making that are more securely rooted in our religious and social traditions. Finally, because we believe that education with a little humor is the most effective kind, we will try to slip in a little chuckle now and then.

CHAPTER 2

Sexual Moral Norms: What Does It Mean?

Katherine is a 23-year-old woman from a traditional religious background. She is currently a law student but does not want to think about marriage until she graduates. She has been in love with Bob since they met in college. They have always been very sexually attracted to each other, but Katherine's religious commitment has compelled her to postpone having intercourse until she was married. Although Bob's religious views are not as strong, he has agreed to defer to Katherine's wishes. Now Katherine is having some second thoughts as to whether or not to have sex with Bob. Bob is in the military and does some highly dangerous actions in the line of duty. He feels it would not be fair to Katherine to marry her until he is transferred to a safer assignment. He is about to go off on a fairly lengthy and dangerous assignment. Katherine is sure she wants to marry him eventually and be the mother of his children. If he should not return from this mission, she will never have the child she wants from him. If she has sex with him before he goes, it will be a sin. If she elopes, it will break her mother's heart. If she has a baby and Bob does not return from the mission, that child of love will be born out of wedlock. She realizes that she is very confused. She is in the center of a moral, ethical and value dilemma. Even discussing the subject with someone is difficult because she is not able to assess the relative weight of her conflicting morals, ethics and values.

We cannot suggest a solution for Katherine. She herself must find the road that she must take. However, how we can help in this chapter and in the rest of the book is to steer people in the right direction. To do this, we present, where possible, a clarification of the different dimensions that must go into the decision-making process and to repeat over and over that sexual choices based upon impulse, feeling and passion alone without the considerations of their moral and ethical background and consequences may prove to be most destructive. Thus, before we can delve into our explorations of the morality of specific sexual behaviors, we have to let you know what we mean by morals, ethics and values. Where do they come from and what changes are taking place? In a world of ever-increasing and ever-changing choices, what role do they play in shaping our attitudes and guiding our behaviors?

By **morals** we mean a set of lofty principles, usually given to us through the ages by our great religious leaders and philosophers and that have withstood the test of time. These are the guidelines that serve as the basis for determining right from wrong in situations that are not always clear to us. Sociologists have called these *moral norms*, that is, rules for moral behavior that have been with us for a long time and are approved by the institution out of which they emerged—the institution of religion. Katherine's religious upbringing has taught her two important moral norms that bear on her dilemma: to honor and respect her parents and to limit sexual behavior to the marital bond. Although important to her, these norms are apparently insufficient to solve her problem.

Because of the emphasis our society places upon the separation of church and state, some moral norms have become embodied in our secular laws, such as in the criminal codes that define crime in each state. Also, some moral norms that at one time reflected only religious views have been modified

14

by state laws because of different religious interpretations as to whether they are right or wrong. Abortion laws and adultery laws are just two examples.

Ethics are the practical ways of making decisions so that we can determine if a particular behavior we are uncertain about is right or wrong according to a moral code. Ethical considerations are necessary because the morality of a specific social behavior cannot be judged as an isolated act; we must also consider the social context in which it occurs. Ethics help us evaluate the morality of social behaviors by taking other information into consideration. Take killing for example. The Bible commands us not to kill. If one person takes the life of another, it may be difficult to judge the morality or immorality of that act unless we knew the ethical context within which it is done. If a man coldbloodedly takes the life of a shopkeeper during a robbery because he does not want the shopkeeper to identify him later on, we can easily determine that this is murder and therefore an immoral act. On the other hand, consider a police officer confronting a robber who has just killed two innocent people. The robber refuses to surrender his gun and even shoots at the officer. Almost everyone would agree that it is ethical for this police officer to then draw his own gun and shoot the robber in order to protect other innocent bystanders as well as himself even if he has to kill the robber. In this case, he might even be considered a hero because he has endangered his own life in the line of duty.

These two cases may be fairly clear illustrations of unethical and ethical—immoral and moral—behavior, but a recent and now famous trial in New York City presented a much less clear situation. The facts were clear: A young man, Bernhard Goetz, shot four other young men on a subway because he believed they were going to rob and possibly hurt him. It was not clear, however, whether Goetz acted in an ethical manner of self-defense. As it came out during the trial, the value Goetz placed upon protecting himself weighed heavily on his conscience as he contemplated having to behave in what he felt was an

15

uncivilized manner. The public was divided on the issue, but when the case was brought before a court of law for a final judgment, the jury ruled in Goetz's favor with a verdict that the State of New York had not proved beyond a reasonable doubt that he had acted unethically—illegally in this case. While very few persons maintained that the shootings were moral, the judgment seemed to be that they were not immoral either.

Although such issues of life, death and murder may seem far removed from our daily lives, in some respects they are analogous to conflicts and torments people face daily, even in the area of sexual behavior. Katherine believes that her love for Bob is so great that she wants to express this in a sexual manner and that she would welcome the gift from God should she become pregnant. Some might say that the ethical thing to do would be to elope or to have sex with Bob since they are likely to marry. But that would violate the two moral principles in which Katherine believes.

Ethical considerations often conflict with moral principles when a woman faces the decision to have an abortion. She may believe that interrupting the fetal development is murder. At the same time, the pregnancy may be the result of a rape, and both the pregnancy and the child may become daily reminders of the horrendous act. Or, the pregnancy may be the result of an abusing and hateful spouse who forced himself on his wife. Or, the young woman may be only 15 and afraid to face insensitive and abusive parents who are not even aware that she has been sexually active. In other words, we cannot ignore the passions or other values that come to bear in the individual's mind during the decision-making process, just as in the Goetz case. The value these women place on life is being weighed against other values concerning the consequences of bringing an unwanted child into the community and in some cases possibly harming the mother's emotional growth and development.

Still another example: A young girl anguishes: "I know it is wrong to have sex before marriage, but I have such strong sexual feelings for Tom. Why are my God-given feelings to engage in sex wrong when love is such a beautiful thing?" She goes on to say to herself: "Is it right to hurt my boyfriend and me by not having sex when we plan to marry soon?"

You see, it is easy to know what is morally right—or is it?

And now we come to something we have already touched upon in the past few paragraphs: **values**. Values are related to but not the same as morals or ethics. By values we mean the worth, the emphasis, the "value" we place on a particular behavior or symbol or material thing relative to something else. Thus, we may know that something is immoral according to our religious beliefs, but we may place a greater value or importance on that behavior and choose to engage in it even though it does violate what we were brought up to believe is right.

Values influence nearly every aspect of our social behavior— from the very mundane to the most far-reaching. The career we choose, the kind of car we drive, the type of people with whom we associate, and even the sorts of food we eat are all reflections of our values. Indeed, when we try to understand social behavior, we find values are often more influential factors than morals or ethics in shaping our day-to-day behavior. This is true even when we are aware that our values may be in conflict with the moral standards that we are supposed to subscribe to by virtue of our religious upbringing. Often this can be understood by realizing that values may be more tied to feelings, impulses and irrational forces in the human psyche that are related to the particular situational experience and how we are perceived by other people—that is, the values we project to others—idealistic, materialistic, aesthetic and others— are often the bases for how we project *ourselves* to others and want them to think of us. In this way, values are very active in our daily lives, while moral codes may be learned and remain dormant in the absence of continuous social reinforcement by the people around us, our peers and significant others. So it appears that values, which are often very changeable, can have

17

more of a day-to-day influence over us than our moral and ethical beliefs. We will explore this in greater depth with our participants, later in the book.

What is meant by values—by _traditional values_? How do they or don't they reflect our religious beliefs? What is it about these values that we communicate to our children? How come some of us follow the values of our parents and others do not? How come some religious people go to church and synagogue and follow the moral teachings while others go to church and synagogue and do not follow the moral teachings?

While it would be worthwhile to write about all morality and values relating to life and death, war and peace, etc., we are going to concentrate on those values relating to sexual matters. This is not only because of our own professional interests but also because we know that these are the values we learn the earliest, and usually the ones about which people seem the most emotionally concerned and confused. We are not trying to suggest that these are the most _important_ issues in life, but certainly the most _common_. If we cannot deal effectively with choices in these areas on a day-to-day basis, how can we expect people to grapple with the more complex moral issues of war and human survival that we face as a nation and as a civilization? We will suggest in this chapter that learning a moral code in the area of sexual behavior at a young age serves as a paradigm, or model, for the learning of more subtle moral codes needed in a complex social and international world.

Another facet of values which affects us on a day-to-day basis has to do with the behavior of our politicians and other public figures, which at times seems to lack what many consider to be traditional values. Perhaps it is only the result of increased media attention, but this year of 1987 has seen some of our best political and governmental servants behaving in ways we may view as unethical and, to some observers, immoral. Religious leaders, educators, military persons and others in the spotlight, as well as many who do not come to public attention, seem to be faltering when it comes to making correct moral

18

choices or seem unable to think through to the possible outcomes of their choices. As a result of the right choices, some persons may be carried to the heights of civilized creativity and love. But for others, the wrong choices can result in a tragic waste of the gift of life for individuals as well as for nations.

Barbara W. Tuchman, the Pulitzer Prize winning historian, recently wrote a disturbing piece concerning what she sees as the deterioration of ethics in the United States. In it she says:

> It does seem that the knowledge of a difference between right and wrong is absent from our society, as if it had floated away on a shadowy night after the last World War. So remote is the concept that even to speak of right and wrong marks one to the younger generation as old-fashioned, reactionary and out of touch.[1]

In May 1987, *Time* magazine ran a cover story on ethics, titled "What's Wrong?" Two short quotations from this excellent article, which was mostly about political, governmental and business ethics, are also relevant to our discussion:

> In a recent poll for *Time* conducted by Yankelovich Clancy Shulman (. . . based on a telephone survey of 1014 adult Americans conducted January 19–21 . . .) more than 90% of the respondents agreed that morals have fallen because parents fail to take responsibility for their children *or to imbue them with decent moral standards.* [emphasis ours]

> Says ethicist Daniel Callahan, co-founder and director of the Hastings Center think tank near New York City: "When most people talk about morals, they are concerned with laws and regulations and codes." When laws do not exist to regulate a

---

[1] Tuchman, Barbara W. "A Nation in Decline?" *New York Times Magazine.* September 20, 1987, p. 142.

particular situation, "we assume it is pretty much every person for himself."[2]

It appears to many persons that morality has given way to ethics in the political, governmental and business communities; that is, instead of enduring principles of right and wrong being the bases of decision making, practical considerations of right and wrong are being employed that have as their bases not moral principles but what is ethical. And, what is so often meant by ethical is what is acceptable to the community of one's peers. The dangers of this should not be minimized. Many persons who were in the military and were accused of engaging in atrocities against civilians have used this as an excuse: "I was being a good soldier by carrying out the orders of my superiors." The acceptance of one's peers took precedence over higher levels of morality.

We suggest consideration of the following thesis: If one does not learn to translate moral principles into day-to-day ethical considerations in light of social values, then one is like the proverbial ship without a rudder, but with a captain who *believes* the rudder is working.

So what does all this have to do with sex? We believe the earliest and the most pervasive use of morality is in the areas related to the body and sexuality. If schools leave the teaching of sexual moral issues to the churches and synagogues, and the churches and synagogues leave it to the parents, then the burden weighs heavily on the parents. Furthermore, if this teaching fails, the model for learning how to integrate morality in all aspects of life may be missing as the child moves into adulthood.

If our moral code is largely a product of our religious upbringing, how do we acquire our values? Some races and ethnic groups are often credited with doing exceptionally well academically, as if there were some kind of magical property

---

[2] Shapiro, Walter. "What's Wrong?" *Time*, May 25, 1987, pp. 26–27.

transmitted through the genes that produced this. The reality is that these people are not genetically endowed, they excel because they work harder. From an early age, the value they place on becoming successful in life compels them to defer gratifications that may ultimately impede their goal. Thus, they choose to read a book rather than go to a horror movie, to not waste their time in unproductive drug taking and drinking behaviors, and they choose productive leisure time activities, like hiking and model building, instead of passive TV watching. It is easy to say that these youngsters learned these traits and habits from their parents or from their religious or educational leaders, but is this true? Is this the only way in which some of the most important values in life are transmitted? As we will learn from our participants, it is not that simple.

Let us take a closer look at the important role of values for both the individual and society and how all this relates to the real-life sexual situations in which persons often find themselves. At the risk of sounding too preachy: It seems to us that the people who succeed and end up as relatively happy people are the people who for the most part have been in control of their lives in a way that is consistent with the basic values of society. Those who end in tragedy and misfortune seem to be those who have allowed themselves to lose control and/or attempt to react to loss of control by behaving with values that are inconsistent with the basic values of society.

Some of the most destructive situations we see stem from what is sometimes called "sexual politics." In these situations, the main issue is one of control and manipulation, which creates interpersonal problems related to sexual behavior. These people don't have any problems of sexual functioning, but their relationship is a power struggle that often affects their sex life. It seems that either they are in control of their personal and sexual lives or they allow themselves to be controlled by others. When someone is talked into having sex with another when there are nagging doubts in the back of the mind, something has broken down or is not working properly. This, we believe, is often the result of weak and inconsistent moral and ethical decision making brought on by an inability to make the best *choice* based upon ethical considerations.

Many of us would like to believe in the romantic notion of a woman being swept off her feet by her first glance at a young man and falling hopelessly and madly in love as a consequence. In this romantic view of love, the relationship is supposed to be based upon irresistible forces and the woman, as well as the man, is not in control; both act without deliberation in the choice of having or not having sex. In this fantasy world, one does not build a relationship leading to love, one "falls in love," a little like slipping on a banana peel. While many people would like to believe in this fiction—witness the enormous popularity of romance novels in this country and elsewhere—it is necessary for us to point out that attributing the behavior to passion or irresistible impulses is often little more than an excuse for not having thought out in advance what the best choice of behavior should be and then acting wisely to engage or not to engage in that course of action leading to sex. For many people, passions have become a substitute for values in the choice of mates.

Despite this apparent disregard for values among those who seem to fall blindly in love, most people *are* concerned and many are confused about their subsequent sexual activity. They would like to believe that what they have done or are doing is right for them *and* moral as well. This is one of the major concerns that we have noticed in our study of the letters and calls that come into the *Dr. Ruth* radio and TV shows as well as the letters that come to the newspaper column by Ruth Westheimer. Although it has become almost unfashionable to talk about it these days, most people do have a conscience and, therefore, do have sexual concerns. Fortunately, when most of us do something that we know is wrong, we tend to feel a sense of guilt. Of course, right and wrong are not always that clear cut and obvious; if it were, our letters and calls to the stations would not include so many requests for validations of different kinds of sexual behaviors as normal.

For example, a letter from a 16-year-old girl says that she has not yet had a boyfriend and wonders:

> . . . how it is to be in love with someone? I often read romance novels and teenage paperback books to try and get a feeling of what it would be like to have sex with real meaning. I would like to wait until I am married to a good man.
>
> Could you please tell me if it is normal to try to give yourself orgasm through your vagina and to have weaknesses toward very attractive men that are either younger or older than myself?

What this girl, and many like her, is saying is that she sees herself as basically a good person but is confused as to what is right and what is wrong. As we have indicated earlier, something may have gone wrong, not in her as a person, not with her ability to feel or to think, but with the development of her value system. Changes in the loyalties, allegiances and beliefs she was taught in her earlier childhood have resulted in her being confused. For some, an act such as masturbation may be carried on with guilt because they do not know whether or not what they are doing is a sin. Obviously, one cannot apply any hedonistic principle to validate the behavior, for example, "If it feels good, do it," because that has some rather dangerous ramifications. If the young lady just quoted came from a background in which she was taught by her religion that masturbation is immoral or sinful, and yet she wishes to be a virgin until marriage, how does she reconcile her bodily urges with her beliefs? The advice to take a cold shower or some similar glib answer is nothing but an insult to her intelligence. On the other hand, if masturbation is not forbidden by her religion, but only by her parents who may have their own problems with the subject, is it fair to impose their problems on her and claim religious legitimacy for their beliefs when this is not so? Many persons we have talked with believe that some sexual practices are a sin according to their religions when this may not be the case at all.

As much as many of us would like to believe that we are creators of our own moral codes, that we can determine what is morally right or wrong for us and that we can ignore the major sources of moral guidelines—namely the religious and humanistic heritage that has been handed down in Western culture through the ages—it is highly unlikely that we can do so and lead good and loving lives. It is not realistic and may even be dangerous for the individual and for society to encourage the sort of thinking that says that we have the right as individuals to determine our own moral codes. Let us take an extreme but hypothetical example. If a man believes that he has the right to determine morality, and he decides that it is morally right to take the life of another because he perceives that the other person is oppressing him, then any person could justify murder by simply stating: "It was morally right for me, and I am the sole determinant of what is right or wrong, not a society, religion or state." Or take a somewhat different situation. If a woman says: "Irrespective of the law, it is morally right for me to use cocaine or marijuana because I believe that the law is wrong," then a simple extension of such reasoning would allow this person the right to violate any law simply because she does not believe that the law is a just one. Thus, if a poor person should decide that poverty is not fair and that wealth is immoral, she could justly conclude that it isn't necessary to obey the law and that "I should be able to take a rich person's property because the laws that protect that property are wrong, not me." Robin Hood may be a romantic hero to some, but civilization cannot survive by each of us doing anything and everything we feel like doing. Obviously, there must be guidelines and rules, but which ones and whose? Here we have a difficult problem to answer and may not do so to everyone's satisfaction, but as the Talmud teaches us: "It is not thy duty to complete the work, but neither art thou free to desist from it." (The Talmud, *Ethics of the Fathers*, II, Mishna 16.) Thus, we will try.

As we have said, historically, the rules that govern most aspects of social behavior and determine if a specific behavior is moral or immoral, right or wrong, came down from the institution of religion—some from people's beliefs and some from the Bible itself. These rules are passed down through the family and communicated to the children, insuring a continuity of values and ethical behavior so as to make for orderly transition from generation to generation. With the rise of the secular state, laws were developed that frequently paralleled religious laws and beliefs in the sexual, marital and family areas. As we became more secularized, particularly in Western culture, the strength of the civil laws became more powerful than the strength of the religious norms. Just as secular societies have changed, the institutions of religion have also changed. They have split, grown diverse and altered major beliefs. What has emerged, particularly in this country, is a multitude of value systems that reflect religious values and beliefs. These exist along with a set of secular laws that often impinge upon sexual behavior and morals.

This muddying of the lines between the secular and the sacred, between secular rules that govern all citizens and religious beliefs that affect only those adherents to one or another of our many religions, is a major factor in causing much of the confusion about individual choices in the area of sexual morality. Nonetheless, in this confused collection of sentiments, there may be a few basic values that most of us can agree upon that may represent, in part, a way out of much of the confusion surrounding the morality of different sexual behaviors. Such values can at least provide a meaningful frame of reference and source of dialogue among the various elements in the population; that is, among the parents, children and religious and secular institutions that are concerned with sexual morality. These basic principles and values will emerge throughout the book as we talk with many people.

Let us look at a few issues that confuse many persons. Is it morally right or wrong to take a drink of liquor? The answer is yes, and no! Is it a sin to eat pork? The answer is yes, and no! Is it wrong to have sex during menstruation? The answer is yes, and no! Is it a sin to masturbate? Again, the answer is an unequivocal yes, and no! We are not trying to waffle or confuse the reader but to point to one of the major reasons for the confusion surrounding social norms in our society— the diversity of religious views. Let us examine the issue of drinking from this perspective and understand that it applies to the other questions as well.

Suppose one was raised with a religion that forbids drinking alcoholic beverages and declares it to be sinful or immoral. If one is a believer and a follower of that religion and wishes to remain a believer and a follower of that religion, then one is forbidden to drink the alcohol. If one does so, one is a violator of the religious norm governing drinking. On the other hand, suppose one grows up as a believer or follower of a religion that says that fruit of the vine is a great gift from God and that it must be used to celebrate the community of followers who believe in God and to celebrate the glory of God. If one then refuses to drink, one would be committing a wrongful, if not sinful, act by refusing what the belief says should be done.

If we all grew up in isolated communities with no exposure to other religious beliefs and value systems, there would probably be little, if any, ambiguity about what is right and wrong. But in our society, where we are exposed to legitimate alternative behaviors in other belief systems, that is, other religions, there is inherent doubt cast on the necessity to adhere to those values that our religion expects us to follow. If good, decent and religious people who come from other faiths can think differently about birth control, premarital sex, homosexual acts and abortion, choices of behavior become more and more difficult to make.

Sometimes, the difficulty arises from not fully understanding either what the position of one's own religion really is or what the implications of violating the religious commitment might be. Gaining this understanding is not always easy. Even within the same religion there may be varying and quite diverse interpretations. For example, there is Orthodox Judaism (the most traditional) as well as Conservative, Reform, and Reconstructionist. Although the Roman Catholic church does not have separate divisions, it has a similar difference of interpretation between the traditional and nontraditional beliefs. There is no apparent traditional viewpoint in modern Protestantism, but the numerous denominations do certainly espouse different teachings. All this can make it difficult for a person properly to understand and follow the position of his or her particular religion.

In our discussions of sexual issues, we will try to present both traditional and contemporary views of the major religious groups. (Our apologies to other groups we have encountered and learned from in our studies but do not have the space to present in this book.) A few general words about these major groups and some of the changes that have occurred may be helpful first. Obviously, we have to oversimplify these next few paragraphs, but these issues will be elaborated upon throughout the book.

The traditional, that is, the Orthodox, Jewish view on sexuality is that sex is limited to a relationship between a husband and wife in the process of creating and raising a religiously observant family. Thus, all forms of sex other than intercourse between husband and wife are forbidden and other issues such as divorce, abortion and masturbation are interpreted and regulated through the biblical Jewish law that the believer must follow. Reform Judaism is much more liberal in allowing the rabbi to interpret the law to be consistent with modern knowledge and the modern secular state. Conservative Judaism is somewhere in between.

The traditional Roman Catholic view on sex holds that the purpose of sexual acts must be for procreation in keeping with a knowable natural law—and the main purpose of procreation is not just bringing a new life into being but also nurturing and educating that life in an observant family context. Thus, such acts as masturbation, using contraceptives, homosexuality, among others, are forbidden since they cannot result in a pregnancy. Even though other acts, such as nonmarital sex and adultery, can result in pregnancy, they are forbidden because they are outside of the marriage and family bond. In 1965, the Second Vatican Council developed a somewhat different perspective on the nature and meaning of sexuality that is still being debated in Roman Catholic circles. This view appears to depart a bit from the clear-cut traditional view of what is or is not acceptable and permits both greater emphasis on the nature of the relationship between the male and female and an examination of a wider range of sexual expressions that might have been automatically considered wrong before. We will see what this means in later chapters.

It is the Protestant perspective we have the most difficulty with because, as we have said, there is no obvious traditional point of view to present as a baseline as there is with Judaism and Catholicism. To help us, we drew upon the work of theologian James B. Nelson, professor of Christian ethics at the United Theological Seminary of the Twin Cities, in Minnesota. Consider this passage taken from his book *Between Two Gardens: Reflections on Sexuality and Religious Experience:*

Protestantism has largely attempted to formulate sexual ethics from biblical grounds. The resultant ethics show a considerably greater variety, coming as they do from a diversity of faith communities with looser patterns of authority in doctrine and morals . . . [than Roman Catholic sexual ethics]. . . . But Protestant ethics perennially have had difficulty in finding a

28

firm grounding for sexual values and norms, and in finding
ways of adjudicating conflicting norms. Protestants, moreover,
have been less clear methodologically. Attempting to affirm the
Bible as primary authority within a plurality of other sources,
mainstream Protestants have discovered that the relativity of
biblical texts and themes has made it difficult to specify particular
rules of sexual conduct and to demonstrate the primacy of the
Bible's authority.

Protestant ethics have thus struggled to find a course between
legalism on one side and normlessness on the other. . . . The
antidote to legalism is an ethics that finds its center and direction
in *love* rather than in a series of specific, absolute injunctions.
Such an ethics takes the Bible seriously, but understands the
need for critical awareness of how its sexual teachings and
practices not only reflect the biblical community's perception of
God's intentions but also reflect sexual mores common to those
historical circumstances.[3]

And Katherine? It is possible that if we knew the relative
value Katherine places on the different components of her
dilemma, we might be able to say which choice (to keep the
relationship as is, to have sex with Bob, or to elope) is least
harmful to all concerned. We would need to weigh the values
she places on keeping her religious commitment to remain a
virgin until marriage, her physical love urges for Bob, her
desire to have his child should he be killed, respect for her
parents' wishes to have a church wedding, the stigma of unwed
motherhood, the possible interference with her education if
she becomes a mother, and so forth. Will she take all the moral,
ethical and value issues into consideration before acting? We
hope so. Do we realistically expect her to? No, unfortunately,
she probably has not had the training in such complicated
decision making. Another reason why we are writing this book!

Sadly, we cannot offer any quick and easy solutions to the

[3] Nelson, James B. *Between Two Gardens: Reflections on Sexuality and Religious Experience*,
New York: Pilgrim Press, 1983, pp. 80–81.

problems and issues we have presented in this chapter and will discuss throughout this book. Our hope is that we can clarify them a bit and put them in a better perspective. As a start, recall the thesis we proposed in Chapter 1: If one does not learn to translate moral principles into day-to-day ethical considerations in light of social values, then one is like the proverbial ship without a rudder, but with a captain who *believes* the rudder is working.

Or, as we put this in another way in this chapter: The people who succeed and end up as relatively happy people are the people who for the most part have been in control of their lives in a way that is consistent with the basic values of society. Those who end in tragedy and misfortune seem to be those who have allowed themselves to lose control and/or attempt to react to loss of control by behaving with values that are inconsistent with the basic values of society.

O.K., let's see if we can help clarify these issues a bit in the following chapters.

CHAPTER 3

Masturbation: Teaching Morality in the Cradle

All of us who have had younger brothers and sisters or who took responsibility for changing a baby's diaper know that even the youngest children seem to love to fondle and play with their genitals. And, judging from the smiles and cooing sounds many of them make while doing so, they appear to be giving themselves a great deal of pleasure. The boys get erections while doing this and, as some pediatricians believe, girls may give themselves orgasms.

Despite the pleasure that their child may be having, many parents seem to be bothered by this behavior and try to make the baby stop. Very likely, the first moral teaching concerning sexual behaviors we experience has to do with masturbation, and it generally begins when we are mere infants. Some parents will slap the child's hand and firmly say: "No! That's bad for you!" (as if the child were capable of understanding). Others will try to divert the child's attention to something else, by offering a toy or food. Some parents may carry this to an extreme by bundling the child under the blankets and fastening the blankets with diaper pins in such a manner that he or she cannot touch this source of pleasure. And there are even some who threaten to "cut if off" should they notice their 3- or 4-

31

year-old son masturbating. We do not mean to suggest that we want children masturbating on public streets, but it does seem to us that many parents, if not most, are overly concerned about this.

We share the belief of many of our colleagues that impressions made on and associations made by even a very young child can have a lasting effect on the emotional development of the child, and may carry through to the adult years. Try to imagine what must go through the innocent mind of a child who is giving himself or herself pleasure only to gradually learn that such pleasure is bad, dirty, wrong and forbidden. These prohibitions are rudimentary moral lessons for a child. Unfortunately, these messages are simple, negative learning experiences in which a child begins to associate the pleasure of his or her genitals with something vaguely bad. Such negative associations may cause long-lasting, and sometimes severe, psychosexual damage to a child that should not be ignored. These consequences have only recently been studied by such eminent researchers as John Money, Professor Emeritus of medical psychology and pediatrics at Johns Hopkins University.

For some, this early association of forbiddance with that which is pleasurable can be a lifelong model for the "forbidden fruit." If something is forbidden (but we can't understand why or what is really wrong with it) it must be pleasurable, or else, why would it be forbidden? Although they may not surface, the old memories are there in which forbidden was equated with pleasure. Consequently, many people assume that if something is forbidden, it must be pleasurable. Even though we are talking mainly about a young child's mind, not the rational mind of an adult, such associations are not uncommon among adult substance abusers. It appears that the more forbidden a drug is, the more some people seem to believe that it is likely to give them "pleasure." Placebo studies, in which people have been given inert substances that they thought were active and then got "high" or drunk, have tended to confirm this. We should not underestimate the power of our

32

beliefs and our minds to create what may at first appear to be a physical response. That is why Ruth Westheimer has so often said that the mind is the best aphrodisiac.

Why are adults so concerned about the masturbation of children? For most, it is still a very difficult subject to talk about, even for those in therapy. We have found that negative attitudes concerning masturbation seem to be rooted in two orientations: first, beliefs that it is harmful, and second, beliefs that it is immoral.

Few people today would still hold to the beliefs that many of us were told as we were growing up in Europe and America:

- Masturbation causes blindness.
- Your uncle went insane from too much masturbating.
- Women grow facial hair because they masturbate.
- Men who masturbate will grow hair on the palms of the hands.
- You will get consumption (tuberculosis) from masturbating.

These folktales seem to be related to a slightly higher level of misinformation: A man has a limited amount of this "precious body fluid," and if too much is used up, he will be weakened and subject to physical deterioration. We laughed at this nonsense presented in the movie *Dr. Strangelove*, when a military officer seemed obsessed with preserving his "body fluids." Yet, many of us were taught this in some of the most respected institutions during the 1940s, including physical education courses in our public school and even in the *Boy Scout Handbook*. The latter told of the necessity not to "abuse" the body (in those days, "self-abuse" was a euphemism for masturbation) in the chapter on conservation of natural resources. We conserve our forests, we protect our seas, we save our semen. (Pardon the unintentional pun.)

The *Boy Scout Handbook* may be looked upon as a barometer of moral values in America and how they have changed over the years. Back in 1916, in the chapter "Health and Endurance"

33

written by a physician, we find this view expressed under a subheading "Conservation":

> In the body of every boy who has reached his teens, the Creator of the universe has sown a very important fluid. . . . This fluid is the sex fluid. . . . Any habit which a boy has that causes this fluid to be discharged from the body tends to weaken his strength, to make him less able to resist disease, and often unfortunately fastens upon him habits which later in life can be broken only with great difficulty. Even several years before this fluid appears in the body such habits are harmful to a growing boy.[1]

Robert Francoeur, the author of many books on sexual behavior, points out that a negative view of masturbation reflects community values, and that changes in those values have been reflected in the *Boy Scout Handbook*:

> The 1934 edition of *The Boy Scout Handbook* included a paragraph on "sex fluid conservation." This section of the *Handbook* implied that any "habit" that causes a boy to lose "fluid" from the body tends to weaken him and makes him less resistant to disease. [Note that this is the same attitude expressed in the 1916 edition.] A 1948 edition of this *Handbook* states that occasional masturbation is wrong and such habits should be broken. Twenty years later, in 1968, the *Handbook* asserted that masturbation may cause sexual guilt and worries and, therefore, should be carefully avoided. Responding to a new understanding of sexual development, the 1978 edition simply avoids the topic and advises boy scouts with questions to talk with their parents, minister, or physician about any sexual concerns they may have.[2]

---

[1] Fisher, George J. "Health and Endurance," in *Boy Scouts of America: The Official Handbook for Boys*, Fifteenth Edition, New York: Doubleday, Page & Co., 1916, pp. 318–319.

[2] Francoeur, Robert T. *Becoming a Sexual Person*, New York: John Wiley, 1982, p. 663.

It seems probable that the changes of attitude reflect the research knowledge that masturbation is nearly universal and does not have harmful physical or psychological consequences. By 1978, we can see a subtle recognition that this is probably a religious or moral issue; thus, the "passing the buck" to the family and church (alas, they still couldn't let go of the physical harm notion and kept the doctor in). Did the family and church carry out their responsibility? We will see.

Those who base their negative attitudes upon the issue of morality cite a vague reference to the biblical story of Onan and his "spilling of the seed" (Genesis 38:8–9)—hence the word *onanism* meaning masturbation.[3] But if you ask them why that should make it immoral or even wrong, a vagueness of response may force the answer: "Well, the semen was meant only for the production of babies." To this we respond: "But why, then, did God give young men the capacity for nocturnal emissions, over which they have no control?" At this point, our moral dialogues usually end.

Where did these beliefs come from in our culture?

For most of the history of Western culture, attitudes, beliefs, knowledge, regulations and punishments for sexual immorality have centered primarily around the Roman Catholic church. Even though the source of the beliefs may have evolved from the biblical Hebrews (who may have taken some of their beliefs from earlier religions and cultures), the dominant position of the church in the early and late Middle Ages set the tone for what followed through the centuries.

For example, in the fifth century, St. Augustine took the position that anything outside of the "natural" use of sexual intercourse for procreation was a sin against nature itself. Later, as with many other "sins," such sexual acts entered the

---

[3] It is interesting to note that, according to biblical scholars, the story of Onan probably referred to *coitus interruptus*, that is, Onan withdrawing before ejaculation and failing to fulfill his social and religious duty to impregnate the widow of his brother, rather than to masturbation.

criminal codes of different countries as "crimes against nature." Masturbation often fell into this category because it appeared to be a sexual act, that is, it involved a sexual organ but not in its "natural" form. The use of the penis for urination is "natural," but for pleasure—as opposed to procreation—it must be "unnatural." In a like manner, for a woman to pleasure herself using her sex organs was "unnatural" and thus a sin. As the religious literature of this period tells us, harsh penances were given for masturbation, when it was discovered—more so for adult males than for young boys or girls.

As we moved into the Age of Reason at the end of the seventeenth century, and the influence and control of religion in political and intellectual life was weakening, so too was the religious control over sexual behavior and norms. Thus, the philosopher Jean-Jacques Rousseau could write that he often satisified his sexual desires through masturbation because that was to him morally acceptable. But at the same time, he did think that too much masturbation might be harmful.

By the early eighteenth century, medical literature began to appear claiming that masturbation might damage memory; that the body would waste away through loss of such body fluids as semen unless it was periodically restored; that semen was needed for masculine development to cause the beard to grow and muscles to thicken. One could have intercourse, *occasionally*, but masturbation was sure to lead to almost every malady from pimples to insanity. And, this was not only true for men but for women as well, although the types of problems they could develop were more related to "female disorders."

Not too long after this, the influential Swiss physician Simon André Tissot gave respectability to a medical theory of degeneracy due to masturbation.[4] As John Money noted:

---

[4] For an insightful and amusing account of the lengths to which some of our most famous citizens went to promote an antisexuality set of attitudes in the name of medicine, read Money, John. *The Destroying Angel: Sex, Fitness and Food in the Legacy of Degeneracy Theory, Graham Crackers, Kellogg's Corn Flakes and American Health History*, Buffalo, N.Y.: Prometheus Books, 1985.

To be logically systematic, Tissot needed to fit women in onanistic degeneracy theory. "The secretion which they lose, being less valuable and less matured than the semen of the male, its loss does not enfeeble so promptly . . . (but) . . . the symptoms are more violent."[5]

When the psychologists entered the picture, they did little to correct all this misinformation, but instead added some of their own. The pioneer American psychologist G. Stanley Hall believed that masturbation was "caused" by older children who seduced their younger siblings or friends. Richard von Krafft-Ebing, a Viennese psychiatrist who published his classic *Psychopathia Sexualis* in 1886, thought that masturbation was the cause for almost anything deviant. He also regarded it as "psychopathic," as he did all sex that did not lead to procreation.

Today, most of us who work professionally in the areas of human sexuality and medicine would reject the unscientific or pseudoscientific pronouncements about the medical or psychological dangers of masturbation. On the contrary, sex educators and sex therapists understand the normalcy of masturbation in the sexual development of the young and the usefulness of masturbation as an aid to the sexual interaction between two loving persons or when one is deprived of having a sexual partner. We even encourage the use of masturbation in the treatment of some sexual dysfunctions.

Although the "scientific" antipleasure attitudes that preceded the Victorian age and seemed to support the older religious moral perspectives on the sinfulness of onanism, "the spilling of the seed," can today be refuted by modern medicine and psychology, this does not mean that the religious/moral interpretation is totally invalid. On the contrary, from a religious perspective, the act of masturbation may be held to be immoral because it is part of a larger system of morality even though it is not harmful to anyone. As Rabbi Leonard Kravitz, professor

---

[5]*Ibid.*, p. 52.

of homiletics (theological preaching) at Hebrew College–Jewish Institute of Religion, told us:

> Masturbation is an act concerning the control of the body by the individual and that is the key issue as to whether or not it concerns the religious system. . . . An important point to remember is not that the semen is wasted, because even if a person masturbated but not to the point of ejaculation that still would not be permitted by traditional Jewish beliefs. In one sense, it is the possibility of pleasure when touching the penis which would define the act as immoral because it could lead to the next stage of intercourse outside of marriage. So you see, the notion of pleasure leading to the loss of control was considered horrendous. Remember, in traditional and conservative religious systems, once you lose control you may be given over to everything. If you can allow the loss of control in anything, the religious system working in you is in danger and therefore the community of religion is in danger.
>
> To try to understand why Judaism, and later Christianity, developed what appears to be an antisexual and anti-sexual-pleasure set of attitudes, we must remember that Judaism developed during a period of the ascendancy of fertility cults. To the ancient Jews, their "old time religion" was probably a fertility cult. In this context, we can speculate that control of sexual behaviors was a religious theme to keep the emerging new religion from sliding back into the temptation of fertility cults.

We found this perspective very revealing in light of the many sexual behaviors, including masturbation, that children are conditioned to control at the earliest stages. All the "don'ts" and all the "no-no's" reinforce what is apparently a moral perspective of self-control. They are not merely for the convenience or embarrassment of the "uptight" parents or for old-fashioned customs as some people may feel. It is unfortunate that the process of controlling masturbation is so often linked with an antipleasure attitude that goes far beyond the principle

N.B.

of learning self-control. On the contrary, if we did not start with the assumption that pleasure is threatening to moral systems, we could learn to control pleasure and make it an appropriate support to moral systems. But then, we would have to teach responsible pleasure as we now teach restraint. Is our world ready for this level of maturity?

To be fair to contemporary religion, we must point out that today very few, if any, religious leaders in Western culture would say that sexual pleasure, for example masturbation, is wrong *per se*, but the context within which it occurs is crucial to this determination. More on this later.

Another religious perspective on the moral aspects of masturbation was told to us by Father Finbarr Corr, a Roman Catholic priest:

The position of the Roman Catholic church has become more complex. From a traditional point of view, masturbation is a sin, both for women and men. If someone were to ask a priest years ago only if it was or was not a sin, that would have been the reply.

You see, before the Second Vatican Council and the publication of *The Church in the Modern World* in 1965, the church focussed more on the physical act itself and it appeared from the writings that pleasure was tolerated only because of the good that was done in procreating children, and sex for pleasure alone was considered a venal sin. But in the Second Vatican Council, the church took the position that sex in itself is a good and holy thing, within the context of a marriage and a husband and a wife making love to each other. Therefore, pleasure is not merely tolerated now but is considered good if part of the process of working toward procreation. However, now, what is more likely to happen is that someone will ask me if he is guilty of sin should he masturbate when his wife is sick or he is out of town, I would tell him that that would minimize the culpability.

But masturbation does not always mean the same thing to all parishioners. For example, I would define masturbation as fondling the genitals to the point of ejaculation or exciting

39

oneself even without ejaculation. Complications arise when someone wants to know if fondling one's own gentials to excite his wife during a loving sexual experience constitutes masturbation. In this case, it would not be masturbation if it were foreplay leading to normal intercourse but would be if it were done without leading to sexual intercourse. The same is true for women—for the wife to excite herself and to reach orgasm without intercourse being the intended goal would be an act of masturbation.

Therefore, what is usually thought of as masturbation, and oral sex as well, may not be a sin if the intention is for it to be part of a process in which the husband deposits his seed inside his wife so that there is a possibility of the creation of a new life. Otherwise, these acts would be sins. However, if the husband should unintentionally ejaculate in his wife's mouth, this would not be a sin. So you see, intention is an important consideration to determine if an act is sinful or not.

While the traditional values of Judaism and Christianity dominated thinking about the morality or immorality of masturbation, both religions changed and evolved over the centuries and gave rise to reformation and subdivisions so that now we have different branches of Judaism and many denominations in Protestantism as well as other branches of Christianity. It would be tedious to most readers to go through the positions of each group on the issues involved in masturbation and morality (and this book would never be completed). What we are more directly concerned with stems from the assumption that all religions have a perspective on the permissibility of masturbation and all the other sexual acts we will discuss. For children being raised with a religious identification whose parents want them to behave in a moral fashion befitting their religion, the methods and thoroughness by which they learn their religion's sexual standards can be extremely important. After all, if parents want their children to have high moral standards in sex as in all other areas of life, then the teaching must be adequate. But who should teach morals and ethics and

40

values? We hear this controversial question raised almost daily in the press, courts and floors of Congress. Should the schools teach morals or should we leave it, as always, to the churches and synagogues? Or, should it be left to those closest to the children—the parents? Let's begin by looking at what some of our respondents told us about how they were (or were not) taught sexual moral standards regarding masturbation. First, a young woman, 25 years old:

> My earliest recollection about masturbation was not of it being right or wrong, but, then, I had these older brothers who were constantly playing with themselves; so I grew up with people masturbating near me. I never heard anybody at home—my parents or my brothers—or anybody in the synagogue or Jewish Community Center ever telling me, or ever telling my brothers for that matter, that masturbation was wrong or a sin or anything like that. I never talked about anything related to sex with my mother until I was 13. However, by the age of 5, my brothers were already telling me what was going on, not whether it was right or wrong.
>
> But at the age of 13, one evening, out of the clear blue sky, my mother turned to me while we were watching TV and said: "Sheila, do you know how to masturbate?" I remember I was stunned because I thought she was going to ask me what show I wanted to watch next. I was so stunned she had to repeat the question. Then I stuttered and stammered with a "No, probably not, not really," and she responded with: "If you ever want to learn, just ask me." I said: "O.K." and that was the end of any discussion of masturbation.

Another female, in her late twenties:

> No, nothing was told to me about whether masturbation was or was not a sin. Nothing from a religious source and certainly nothing from my family. I heard about it at school, from my friends, but that was about what it was and whether we did it. Things like that. Nothing about whether it was a sin or not. As a matter of fact, I first spoke about it with my mother only

recently. We were talking about a friend of mine who had difficulty in her marriage related to lack of orgasm. And my mother confessed, somewhat embarrassed, that she had never had an orgasm in her life. Believe it or not, I had to educate her about masturbating with a vibrator in order to learn how to become orgasmic.

My mother had told me about menstruation and that it's not a curse but a very normal body function. Very little more was said about sex and nothing about morality.

My baby sitter told me a little about the body parts. And that's it. Nothing about whether I should or should not masturbate.

A male in his late twenties who went to parochial school from kindergarten through college:

Even though I was in Catholic schools, I didn't hear any teacher talk about sin in connection with sexual matters. One person, an eighth grade teacher, said that nude pictures of women were "raw" and not very nice. That was all. In the seventh grade, there was one or two references to sex, but they were minor and made no impression on me. For example, someone talked about the sin of Onan and the wasting of the seed, but I really didn't know what they were talking about. We never got any lectures on the "birds and the bees." They seemed to give us the impression that any discussion of sex was our parents' responsibility. But all my mother ever said was: "Don't touch yourself." I didn't know why I shouldn't.

I didn't receive any direction or foundation in those areas until I reached high school. I went to church every Sunday, but I don't recall any sermons on morality and sex. Nobody ever talked about masturbation in church, but I did hear about it from some teachers during my first year in high school. They didn't say it was wrong, only that it wasn't nice, it wasn't the right thing to do. No one said that it was sinful or immoral or against Biblical teaching. I suppose I was fortunate and had an enlightened bunch of brothers at my high school. By my junior year, we were getting a health and sex education course that did not pass judgment on the values of having intercourse, having oral sex or the perils of masturbation. Oh, they talked about them, but they never pushed you into a corner by saying: "This is bad, this is evil, this is against God's word."

A young male told us this amusing story:

I went to Sunday school from the age of 6 until the age of 15. We learned Jewish history and culture, as well as the Hebrew language and training for the Bar Mitzvah. It was not only on Sundays that we went but also a couple of days during the week. However, in all that time, I never heard anyone, rabbi or teacher or anyone else, ever instruct us as to the Jewish position on masturbation. In fact, the first time I heard of Onan I was already in college when an acquaintance mentioned that he had named his bird Onan because he always spilled his seed upon the ground. That was actually the first reference I ever heard to Onan.

It was true that I learned the basic Bible stories, but they were presented in a way which had no connection with me. Yes, we learned about Sodom and Gomorrah but in very vague terms about there being sin there but nothing about the sexual connotations, just that they were sinful.

We never talked about the rightness or wrongness of masturbation in Jewish camps or any other Jewish or non-Jewish settings.

With responses like these, it looks like we are not going to be able to say very much about how people learn their moral values concerning masturbation. Maybe it's because parents, ministers and educators can't believe that the innocent-looking little leaguers, who can't stand being around girls, and the young girls, who say that boys are rough and disgusting, are the same ones who are masturbating under the covers at night. Is it that people don't believe that preteens are sexual beings or is it that they don't want to believe it? We all know of sad cases in which a loving father stops being demonstrably affectionate to his daughter once she gets her period because he

43

thinks that now that she has become "a woman," he must find new ways of relating to her. It is like the father who used to kiss his son on appropriate occasions but just shakes his hand when the boy approaches puberty because now his son is becoming a man, and men don't kiss men. All of this is so sad for the children and reinforces the stereotypes that masculinity and femininity emerge as a result of hormonal changes at the time of puberty. We suspect that many adults base their behaviors toward young children on the belief that sexuality begins in adolescence. If they had to accept the reality of childhood and preteen sexuality, they might feel compelled to behave differently toward their children. Also, accepting the fact that their preteen child is a sexual being could be very frightening to those parents who are trying to grapple with and repress their own sexual feelings toward their children.

Parents may try hard to deny that there is sexual activity of a sort going on, but is there a parent who can deny that his or her own children or neighbor's children have played games of "You show me yours and I'll show you mine," or "doctor and nurse" or "house" when adults are not around? Many parents have had to cope with preteen siblings experimenting with each other sexually, maybe not to the point of intercourse, but in an innocent exploratory way. If parents disapprove of youthful noncoital sexual behavior practiced either alone or together, and if religions teach that such behavior is immoral, should parents avoid discussing it with their children? Do parents refrain from discussing the morality of masturbation with their children because it is in the children's best interest, or is it that parents and other adults are too uncomfortable to face the issues and would rather act like the proverbial ostrich? Unfortunately, we found the avoidance of discussing the morality of masturbation and not allowing the child to learn parental moral values to be the norm rather than the exception among people of all races, ethnic groups and religions. For example, a young woman deeply committed to her ethnic community and church told us:

44

No one in my church or family ever talked about sex or sexual morals and I was very naive about sex even though I was 12 or 13. I really didn't know what was right or wrong until I would hear my friends talk about oral sex, for example—they called it "69"—but I wouldn't understand what they were talking about. Like with masturbation, I wouldn't know what they were talking about and they would laugh at me, so I would ask my best friend and she would tell me.

My parents never brought the subject up so that the only way I knew that it was bad was the way my friends acted about it. That was because they whispered about it. I guess they were masturbating, but we never talked openly about it, not even among my friends.

Now, I feel that masturbation is natural, pleasurable, like eating good food. You swim when it's hot and you feel good. It's like that to me now. I don't know why doing something which feels good is wrong. It's doing something to yourself which doesn't seem to me to be harmful or immoral. It's not like doing drugs or anything else to hurt your body.

Do I think the priest would disapprove? He might. I don't really know what he believes in or the position of the church on this subject. The only time I heard a priest in the Armenian church say something about sexual behavior was in a lecture to an audience of boys and girls on a festive occasion. All he said was that it wasn't "nice" to kiss in public and display private affection in public. He gave this lecture because he had once seen some of us kissing in public. He said it wasn't polite and that it showed a lack of respect.

Another young woman told us:

No one either at home or at the church or my friends' ever said a word about masturbation. I learned about it from a popular book at home on family medical problems. I was about 12 or 13 then and concerned with my weight so I looked at the book and found a discussion on wet dreams and masturbation, but it seemed like it was geared only to boys, and there was no mention of girls masturbating. I realized that it could happen, however.

45

My parents never said anything about masturbation. Recently, my sister had a baby boy and it seems like all he ever does is play with himself. Whenever my mother sees this she says: "Get your hand away from there." But he's only nine months old and can't understand anything. Now I'm conscious of it. Maybe she did that when I was a little kid, too.

Recently, my mother found out that I had read a best selling sex manual. She got upset and said: "That's digusting. Why are you reading that?" I said: "Mom, that's natural. Besides, I'm 21 years old!" I never could talk with my mom about sex. Everything I learned came from my sister or my friends.

So it looks like we can't depend upon parents or religious ministers to discuss the morality of masturbation, even among such intelligent and verbal young persons as we have interviewed for this book. Among the hundreds of persons we have talked with, they report either no discussions or merely confused ones about the rightness or wrongness of this sexual behavior. The very attractive young woman we just quoted went on to tell us, as so many others did, that she had felt very badly and negative about her body when she was young. We cannot say how much of this was due to deeply buried associations that there is something wrong with the body so that it is forbidden to touch it, but we firmly believe that these earliest messages and associations that a child may make, even before the age of two, may have lifelong implications. We base this on recent research about early childhood socialization and about how learning and development during the first two years of life has an important influence on adult personality development. We have no reason to assume that negative messages concerning body image are not also just as important as other learning experiences. As Mary S. Calderone and Eric W. Johnson said in their book *The Family Book about Sexuality*:

No one has ever reassured the mother that not only is it normal for a baby to find pleasure in its own body, but it is also an

46

important part of the baby's growth and development and should not be interfered with. . . .

When a baby discovers its genital organs, it is actually initiating the active functioning of the sexual response system which, years later, will be physiologically ready enough to permit normal sexual functioning accompanied by a sense of competence, fulfillment, and pleasure.[6]

Sometimes a value or moral message does get communicated but it may lead to some confusion and perhaps be inconsistent with contemporary religious teachings. For example, from a woman in her early twenties:

In the parochial school, they didn't exactly say that it was wrong to masturbate. What they told us is that our body is not ours, it is God's and we are not entitled to do anything to it which is not within God's teaching. According to the nuns there, our body is just to procreate and not to be enjoyed. I'm sure that many girls felt very dirty about their bodies, because we were not supposed to touch it, not to use it for pleasure, but only to use it to have children. I'm sure someone there said something about masturbation because that was a taboo.

I still feel that there is something dirty about masturbation. Even though I may now masturbate in front of my husband, I feel uncomfortable or guilty, but at the same time I don't feel it's wrong.

My parents never talked to us about sex but they did tell me not to touch myself!

Even when someone is not told directly, or can't even remember what was said, the messages may be deeply embedded, as this woman told us:

No one ever mentioned anything about masturbation to me so that I didn't even know what it was. I was so dumb about

---

[6] Calderone, Mary S., M.D. and Eric W. Johnson. *The Family Book about Sexuality*, New York: Harper & Row, 1981, p. 21.

masturbation that I had actually had sexual intercourse before I ever tried masturbation. I was so in the dark about it that I was in college before I ever experimented with it. Even then, I felt guilty about it, but I didn't know why. Obviously, someone had said "no" because I felt this guilt. I had this discussion with my mother years ago because she didn't understand why I felt so much guilt about sex since I had gone to a liberal church. She said that she had never done anything to make me feel guilty about sex. But I don't buy that.

And, a young woman from a traditional Latino background told us what she remembered:

My sisters and I were playing one day when we were very young, and one of us held something near her to make it look like she had a penis. My mother said: "What are you doing? Get that off there, you're not a boy." Another time, one of my little cousins, a boy, had to go to the bathroom real bad so he was holding himself because the bathroom was occupied. But after that, when one of the girls did that, she was told: "Don't do that, you're not a boy."

When I grew up, the girl children always had to wear T-shirts and keep themselves covered, but the boys went around nude all the time. Sometimes the adults would make jokes about a boy's penis, like: "Oh, big man," and things like that, but never about a girl.

I never heard anything from a priest or any other person in the church about masturbation being wrong, and from my mother, only not to touch down there, but never why or anything like that.

Were these young women being given moral messages and value teachings, or were they merely subject to antisexual, antipleasure, antifemale and pro-macho values? Intended moral messages, which are not part of an understandable and acceptable moral system, tend to be inconsistent and discriminatory and are almost always insulting to the intelligence of young people. It is as if they were being treated as incapable

48

of understanding what is really involved or being said. To tell a child: "You should not touch yourself down there," is to imply that there is something wrong with "down there." After all, good hygiene dictates that girls and boys must clean and wash their genitalia. If they receive pleasure, they must become very confused at what is happening to them. Do we really want to teach them to feel guilty because they feel pleasure at touching themselves?

This is a very vexing problem for parents who want to do the right thing, both by their religious beliefs and in the best interests of their child growing up to be a healthy adult. On one hand, it is certainly not reasonable to expect parents to allow children to masturbate whenever and wherever they want to. On the other hand, psychotherapists and sexual therapists of all types see the tragedy that often arises in marriages because one or the other spouse has so many guilt feelings about sexual pleasure due to their belief that their sexual organs are "dirty" or "bad," or because they are nonorgasmic due to never having trained the clitoris to respond to stimulation, and so forth. True, today we can help most of the people who come to us with these kinds of problems, but how many marriages have been eroded unnecessarily because there was no real awareness of one's negative sexual attitudes? How much better it would be if there were no need for all this "treatment" of sexual problems in adults!

So, can we have a rational approach, consistent with our religious beliefs, without instilling the notion that sexual pleasure from stimulation of the genitalia is something bad? We'll give it a try.

Let us begin by looking at the act of touching one's genitals (or for that matter, one person touching another's genitals). Sociologists and anthropologists, *and* religious educators as well, tell us that isolated sexual acts such as intercourse, looking at another person who is nude, being looked at in the nude, kissing, touching another's genitals (even of the same sex), inflicting moderate pain and so forth, cannot be said to be

49

moral or immoral outside of the context within which they occur. After all, what religion would say that an act of intercourse between a loving husband and wife could be anything but a moral act? (We will ignore the sometimes odd moral codes of certain historical religious cults that did forbid intercourse.) But, the same act forced on a woman against her will (and from our perspective even if she is married to the man) is clearly immoral and wrong because someone is being hurt. This is also true of the distinction between a wife who is admiring the body of her husband in their bedroom and a woman who peeks into her neighbor's windows to watch a man in the nude, while she is walking her dog.

And pain? The husband who in a loving embrace gives a welcome "hickey" to his wife or who nibbles on her ear and causes a little pain that she may want cannot be compared to a husband who uses pain to force his wife to submit to him. The differences are obvious. But what about touching the genitals? Recall the words of Father Finbarr Corr (which reflect what we believe is a fairly conservative religious position): "What is usually thought of as masturbation . . . may not be a sin if the intention is for it to be part of a process in which the husband deposits his seed inside his wife . . . intention is an important consideration to determine if an act is sinful or not."

What is the intention of a baby who plays with his tiny penis? It is obviously not to culminate in an act of intercourse, but neither is it to "spill his seed." His intention appears to be solely to have pleasure, but, it appears that the more conservative lines of Jewish and Christian tradition might thus conclude that either it is an immoral act or it would be if allowed to continue. Here we must speculate a bit: God (or nature, or the process of evolution, if you are so inclined) gives the innocent infant baby boy and girl the capacity for great sexual pleasure through the genitalia, *not merely at puberty when they have the capacity to procreate, but at birth*. If you believe that there is some meaning and order to life and the bodily organs and functions, then you can't help but speculate that there is some reason for the pleasure to be there before there is a reproductive function for it. There is no ejaculate for the infant boy, but there is an erection (a very hard one as parents all know) and sexual pleasure; and for the girls, there is engorgement of the labia and sexual pleasure. Very likely there are orgasms for both infant boys and girls as well as pre-adolescents of all ages as shown by Alfred C. Kinsey, the pioneer researcher of male and female sexuality in the late 1940s and early 1950s.[7,8]

Let us consider a bit of common sense and a little story told to us by Dr. Victor Lief, a wonderful man and great physician who died many years ago. It seems that a very sophisticated couple had an intellectually precocious son of 4 or 5 years of age of whom they were very proud. He could converse with adults, including the parents' learned friends, about many subjects, but he had one bad habit that used to embarrass his parents. He would sometimes sit and stare out the window for an hour or more looking at the trees, just sucking his thumb and speaking to no one. One day while his parents were having an afternoon cocktail party, the boy (let's call him Paul) came into the living room, went over to the window, sat down in a chair, stuck his thumb into his mouth and just kept staring out the window ignoring everyone in the room. This time Paul's parents decided not to be embarrassed; they ignored the incident but called over a few friends who were professionals in the handling of children: a pediatrician, a child psychologist, a family therapist, etc. They explained to their friends what had been going on and they all walked over to Paul and began to speculate (in psycho-jargon) about what might be going on: progressive autism, status inconsistency of a child in an adult world, retreat into the nonintellectual environment of nature, self-gratification versus social gratification, etc. Paul slowly

---

[7] Kinsey, Alfred C., Wardell B. Pomeroy, and Clyde E. Martin. *Sexual Behavior in the Human Male*, Philadelphia and London: W. B. Saunders Co., 1948, pp. 175–181.
[8] Kinsey, Alfred C., Wardell B. Pomeroy, Clyde E. Martin, and Paul H. Gebhard. *Sexual Behavior in the Human Female*. Philadelphia and London: W. B. Saunders Co., 1953, pp. 101–107.

turned around, took his thumb out of his mouth, looked at them and said: "What's the matter, it *hurts* you?"

If our babies could talk, maybe they would say the same thing every time their parents pulled their hand away from their genitals! The parents may be bothered, but does this hurt anyone—is it a sin? Does this mean that we impose no controls on masturbation over our children? Of course not! As Rabbi Kravitz said earlier: ". . . the notion of pleasure leading to the loss of control was considered horrendous . . . in traditional and conservative religious systems. . . . If you can allow the loss of control in anything, the religious system working in you is in danger and therefore the community of religion is in danger." We do not disagree with this position. But allowing infants and very young children the right to masturbate is not the same as allowing infants and children to urinate and defecate wherever they wish. Adults must control their elimination functions in the best interest of everyone in the community; therefore, *when they are capable of learning it*, we toilet train children to go to an appropriate place for these acts. What we are suggesting here is that there is also an appropriate time to teach the child to learn to *control* masturbation just as he or she must control all sexual impulses according to societal and religious norms. If we believe, as does John Money, that much of what children do as sex play is necessary rehearsal for a healthy relationship as sexual adults, then we might view masturbation in entirely a different sense. Said Professor Money:

> For both boys and girls, erotic/sexual development does not begin at puberty, as one folk dogma would have us believe. . . . Deprivation and punishment notwithstanding, young children do sometimes engage in sexual rehearsal play, even in our culture. . . . In the absence of the necessary evidence, it is not yet possible to argue in favor of an exclusively cultural hypothesis to explain the erotic/sexual rehearsal play of childhood. It is more likely that such play represents yet another of those aspects

of human development for which the way is prepared in prenatal programming, but which cannot be completed without postnatal input from the social environment at an appropriate critical phase of development.[9]

Even though children may be engaging in these "sexual rehearsal" activities, should this be viewed as similar to the sexual play of prepubescents and teenagers? Apparently not, for as the famed Swiss child psychologist Jean Piaget noted, children are not capable of moral reasoning until the ages of 6 or 7. If this is so, then their behavior should not be construed as sinful (immoral). Thus, we cannot equate early masturbation to adult masturbation, and what might be considered sinful for adults of particular religious persuasions cannot be considered sinful for the child. On the contrary, interfering with childhood masturbation, other than training the child not to engage in it in public, so as to follow proper etiquette, may actually be interfering with natural law that impels each child to masturbate. Why are they impelled to masturbate? We discussed this in a telephone conversation with Professor Money and agreed that it probably is in keeping with some larger, very likely inborn, plan or programming. Children learn to respond physiologically as nature intended them to in preparation for growing up as sexually active adults. If this is so, then we have behavior that must at the same time be permitted and controlled.

What we have heard, however, from almost every person we have talked with is that *no one* ever taught them to control masturbation. Since they could not remember what was done to them while they were in the crib or cradle, we can only assume that our respondents were treated like so many other children and punished, threatened, diverted, etc. from behaving as their body seems to intend for them to behave.

---

[9] Money, John. *Love and Love Sickness: The Science of Sex, Gender Difference, and Pair-Bonding*. Baltimore: Johns Hopkins University Press, 1980, pp. 51–53.

The common sense approach then, consistent with most religious teaching, is to allow the infant and very young child to masturbate. If they are doing it out of boredom when they are getting no other stimulation or when they have the urge, so what—"It hurts you?" When they are old enough to begin their training, parents should be able to talk to their children and teach them, like we now do with toilet training (in language that they can understand, of course): "Here in this room, in private, you can do this but not where it is not appropriate."

✓ First parents must believe in their hearts and heads not only that it is not a sin for a child to masturbate, but they also must be able to talk about it during the training process. Herein lies the problem. This subject is so taboo that parents by and large do not want to or cannot discuss the issue. This is borne out by almost all of the respondents we have talked with who couldn't recall any discussion of the subject with their parents or any other significant adult. Incidentally, a reflection of how taboo this subject is: When we checked the spelling of the words in this chapter with the spelling-check program in our computer, we discovered that the word *masturbation* was not included—and the program has an 85,000-word dictionary! We also remember that when Dr. Westheimer was teaching student teachers how to teach the subject of sex education, they established a curriculum together and were asked what the content should be. The word *masturbation* never appeared. Everything from erections to abortion showed up, but not once was masturbation listed.

Not only do adults not talk about masturbation, they generally ignore its existence in young children. The denial of the existence of this behavior in preteens (for which perhaps Freud is partially to blame with his latency period description) has resulted in making this subject taboo and is a prime example of the human capacity for self-delusion. Even the revealing statistics of Kinsey, who we mentioned earlier, did not seem to dispel the average parent's view that their children were not masturbating. This denial persists despite stories we were

54

frequently told of children masturbating in school in second and third grade. A female in her early twenties:

> I remember in second grade, at a Catholic school, one girl was saying that she went into a closet with this boy in the class and everybody laughed at me because I said: "Well, what does this mean?" Then they told me about how they went into the closet with this boy, shut the lights and masturbated each other. This was second grade.

Another female, same age:

> In second grade, one of the boys was playing with himself in class, and the teacher said, right in front of the class: "Stop that, you don't do that, it's dirty."

The teacher is obviously placed in a very difficult situation. Without knowing the values of the home, the teacher must be very careful about giving confusing moral messages while at the same time discouraging inappropriate public display of private behavior. But that it is "dirty"? Is this a healthy attitude for any adult to have about masturbation? Certainly the teacher in a parochial school has more latitude because parents who send their children to such schools do so often because they want the moral values of that religion to be imparted to their children. A teacher may use "natural" opportunities to discuss the relevant moral issues with his or her pupils, but too many teachers in parochial schools are much too embarrassed to discuss sexual moral issues with teenagers or preteens.

What about a prepubescent child giving pleasure to himself or herself? Should a parent discourage such behavior? Here, too, it obviously depends on religious beliefs, but if the child is not yet capable of procreating, then the argument that it is wrong because there is no intent to procreate is hard to justify to a youngster. Since the prepubescent cannot make a baby, and God still gives him or her the ability to have pleasure through masturbation we would have to revert to the issue of self-control as being paramount. If the parents believe that it is better for the child to choose not to masturbate, then this should be discussed with the preadolescent. If it is merely a matter of choice, and not religious conviction, then an argument must be presented to the prepubescent youngster as to why the choice of refraining from masturbation should be made.

It seems to us that the present approach, or rather nonapproach, to this problem is harmful to psychosexual development. Although parents are generally too embarrassed, or perhaps unprepared, to discuss masturbation directly with their children, their repeated threats and diversions prove successful, in some cases, in stopping their children from masturbating. But, oh, at what a price to their children!

CHAPTER 4

Nudity: The Stress of Modesty

Following masturbation, the earliest taboo and sexual moral messages that we learn are about nudity—revealing the genitals. These norms and sexual attitudes seem to affect many people in their adult years. Sex therapists, psychologists and others in the helping professions frequently encounter patients or clients whose problems stem from the shame and discomfort they experience about their own bodies and about how their sex organs appear to others.

One of the few "social laboratories" we have where we can study the effects of sexual norms regarding nudity or the relaxation of these norms is the many nudist camps in this country and elsewhere. Is the body taboo, that is, the belief that public and even familial nudity are wrong, immoral or "indecent," really in the best interest of the moral development of the child, or of adults for that matter?

Many years ago, Lou Lieberman did research on the impact of family nudity on children at about twenty-five nudist camps in the United States. One of the most interesting findings had nothing to do with the children but with the fact that almost everyone said that the reason they continued to go to nudist camps was not because they wanted to look at other nude bodies or be looked at but because it made them feel "relaxed." We guess that a lot of our readers might suspect that these nudists were not telling the truth and were actually ashamed to say that they really went there to look at naked bodies close up. These assumptions turned out to be wrong. Most of these people readily admitted that the main reason they *first* went to nudist camps was precisely because they were curious and wanted to look at naked people. But soon the curiosity wore off, and they continued to go because it made them feel "relaxed." If they were willing to tell the truth about their reasons for first going, we had no reason to believe that they would not also be as frank about why they continued. Other researchers had also reported that relaxation seemed to be the main reason for remaining at nudist camps.[1] That seemed a little too simple an answer to explain the phenomena of social nudism (organized camps for recreation and social activities) and nude beaches in the United States as well as many other countries, especially in Europe.

It seemed that if the relaxation were due to the swimming, playing volley ball and tennis as well as other physical and social activities in the sunlight, the imposition of a little bit of cloth to cover the breasts and genitalia could not interfere with the physical activity that much. Can the slight inconvenience or discomfort of a bathing suit be enough to motivate these people to engage in a socially deviant behavior? It seemed paradoxical that these participants claimed to be more relaxed in the very situation in which most people in society would not feel relaxed at all.

Further research focussed in depth on this apparent contradiction: relaxation in a "normally" anxiety-provoking situation. (Is there a reader who has not had the dream in which he or she was nude in a social situation and terribly embarrassed by it all and looking for either a place to hide or some clothes to

---

[1] Hartman, William E., Marilyn Fithian, and Donald Johnson. *Nudist Society*, New York: Crown Publishers, 1970.

put on?) After talking with many people and questioning them at length about how they feel while nude at these camps, an interesting pattern emerged. A typical response from a social nudist, a young man, was:

> After a few visits here I was still a little bit uncomfortable when my clothes were off. But one weekend, I felt great as soon as I took my clothing off. I can't really describe the feeling, but it was as if a great weight were removed from me and I felt really relaxed, like I never felt before—more like being relaxed because I was free, not relaxed like when you have a beer and watch TV.

A young woman had this very interesting observation:

> The first few times I came here with my husband—he was the one who wanted to come here, not me—these first trips, I felt very uncomfortable. I thought that everyone was staring at me—that the women were comparing their bodies to mine and that the men were looking at my breasts and behind and pubic area with lust. But then one day, the day before we were supposed to go for the weekend, I found myself looking forward to going. I didn't know why, but when I got here and took off all my clothes, instead of feeling uncomfortable and nervous and a little bit ashamed, I felt great.
>
> I thought about it later in the day because I felt so good all day, and then it struck me: "Hey, those men can look at your sex parts and it's O.K. They won't make a pass, their wives don't think I am trying to seduce their husbands, my husband doesn't think I'm a loose women because I let men look at me naked. For the first time in my life, at age 37, I don't have to worry that some guy may look up my skirt or that some pervert may look in my window while I go to the shower. All those years of having to keep my body taboo to every stranger's glance, and here, I find it doesn't make any difference. You can't imagine what a relief that is to a woman unless you've experienced the pressures to always be "modest."

This very insightful remark provides us with the meaning of relaxation for the social nudist. It is not the same as feeling comfortable in the nude with your spouse or lover (although many men and women do not feel comfortable even then) or while your physician examines you. These situations are considered socially acceptable. You were probably taught that they are acceptable from your earliest days when your parents took you to the doctor, or when you realized that Mommy and Daddy were sometimes naked together. But in front of strangers—another "no-no"! At these nudist camps, it seems that the relaxation stems from the suspension of a social norm (to remain modestly clothed in front of strangers) that we all learn during childhood. Next to the disapproval of masturbation, nudity is the earliest learned prohibition for most persons in Western culture. It usually begins when the child is old enough to remove his or her clothing and attempts to run around the house naked following a bath, only to have some concerned grownup come running up from behind with a towel or pajamas.

Think of all the emotional energy that must be expended in a person's life in order to make sure that her legs are together when seated in a subway or other public place when wearing a skirt, that his zipper is closed before he goes to lecture in front of a class (even the students are embarrassed for the professor when he forgets to do so), that all window shades are down when undressing for bed (what would the neighbors think), and so forth. In the nudist camp, people are in front of strangers of both sexes, even children. When a woman gets out of a lounge chair by the pool, people can sometimes even see her labia and vulva, but nothing catastrophic happens! No one sexually attacks her, no one says: "Shame on you," men don't begin to leer and proposition her—what a relief! This is what appears to be the main, underlying factor to explain the great sense of relaxation that comes over people in these camps.

We would suggest that if parents did not make their young children and teenagers feel so self-conscious about the naked body (as was so often reported to us), this pervading fear of being caught in the nude, in an inappropriate manner, would affect adults less. We can't help but believe that such repeated messages about how the body must always be covered, even in front of parents and siblings, helps to create a negative body self-image and, consequently, lowered self-esteem. Many persons who work with problems of youth have come to recognize the social and mental-health implications when young people do not think very highly of themselves. There are even suggestions that the euphoria of drug use is sought by many to overcome these negative feelings about one's self. In our private practices, where we treat people with sexual dysfunctions as well as other interpersonal problems, we see patients who remember feeling uncomfortable about their bodies from childhood on. How much of this can be traced directly back to parental prohibitions is not known, but the frequency with which the people we interviewed suggested this is not insignificant.

A seemingly little thing, yet the issue of modesty is an important one in our culture as in most cultures. While some people and families, even those who would not think of going to a nudist camp, feel comfortable if they are nude among their family or friends, others have a great deal of difficulty with "exposing" their bodies to a physician or even their spouse. Lou Lieberman used to counsel a group of persons with problems of body self-image. One member told the group that in the thirteen years of her marriage she had managed to ensure that her husband never saw her nude. There are also some women who have sexual dysfunctions that in part are related to tremendous anxiety due to a belief that their husband may think that the vaginal area is ugly.

Some of the problems with the issue of nudity appear to be due to beliefs that it is immoral to appear naked or to look at a nude person (other than in the accepted role situations we described earlier). Is it immoral to invite your friends over and then join them in the nude in your hot tub or sauna? How and

61

where did our cultural attitudes regarding social nudity develop? Let's first look at some biblical sources.

Many people think that nudity is shameful and immoral because Adam and Eve felt ashamed and put coverings over the sexual parts of their bodies after they were expelled from the Garden of Eden. It is not that clear or that simple in the Bible. On one hand, although Adam "was naked and afraid" (Genesis 3:10) after leaving the Garden, he and Eve "were both naked . . . and felt no shame" while still there (Genesis 2:25). Apparently, even though they covered themselves, this did not mean they did so because they felt "shame." Also, in Samuel (19:24), nudity is associated with the prophets, such as Saul who prophesized in the nude. King David spied on Bathsheba, the wife of one of his generals, while she was bathing in the nude, but neither was condemned for the specific act—she for not being more careful to be concealed and he for looking—suggesting that nudity and seeing someone nude is not necessarily sinful or immoral. The beautiful poetry of love in the Old Testament, attributed to King Solomon (The Song of Songs: 1-8), seems to revere the female body. On the other hand, Noah's son Ham was cursed for observing his father nude (Genesis 9:21-27). It appears that the father was especially prohibited from appearing nude in front of his sons, but no such ban was mentioned for being nude in front of the daughters. This has led to some scholars arguing that it is a fear of homosexuality that was being expressed and not nudity *per se*.[2] Although there is condemnation of "nakedness" in Leviticus (20:11-21), it all seems to be limited only to potentially incestuous relationships.

Some people believe that the traditional Jewish rejection of social nudity really stems from the story of the Maccabees in the eighth century B.C., which is the basis for the holiday of Chanukah. The evidence for this is that the revolt of the

---

[2] Bullough, Vern L. *Sexual Variance in Society and History*, Chicago: University of Chicago Press, 1976, p. 82.

Maccabees first began with attacks on "Hellenized" Jews, that is, Jews who had adopted the customs of the conquerors of Judea including attending sports events in which athletes prepared and participated in the nude. This public nudity became a symbol of the weakening of the ties of the Jews to their traditional religious roots because these athletic events were often accompanied by what ancient Jews considered pagan religious rites. Remembering what Rabbi Kravitz said in Chapter 3 about the fear of the competition from fertility cults and religions, repressive attitudes concerning nudity seem almost an inevitable response.

In contrast, the ancient Greeks associated physical beauty (that is, the body) with eroticism and with moral good—a far different moral standard from the Jews who considered the law (the Torah) to be the basis of morality. The Greeks' reverence of the penis approached religious adoration because of its power to reproduce. One writer summarized their beliefs.

[They believed that] man should not be ashamed of what God had not been ashamed to create. They carried in religious procession symbols of phallus and pudenda in all innocence, and called the sexual parts that which inspires holy awe.[3]

Ambivalence about nudity, both social and within religious cults and movements that practice nudity in rituals, has continued from the second century A.D. through to the present.[4] Certainly today there is still a great deal of strong feeling about public and familial nudity, and for some it is clearly an issue of sexual morality. Rabbi Kravitz told us:

For traditional Jews this is clearly not to be done. Although servants and slaves, in biblical days as in ancient Rome and Greece, may have been nude, nudity was clearly frowned upon

---

[3] Taylor, G. *Sex in History*, New York: Ballantine Books, 1954, p. 227.
[4] Ilfeld, Fred, Jr. and Roger Lauer. *Social Nudism in America*, New Haven: College and University Press, 1964, pp. 23–40.

for those Jews in ordinary circumstances. The traditional argument is that Adam, prior to the fall, was naked but after the fall had to get dressed, and since we are all fallen creatures, we should be dressed. But the traditional religious issue, elaborated upon by Maimonides, is still that of one acting in any way [that] might cause the possible loss of control in the area of sexuality.

Today, we would rationalize this by giving the psychological answer, namely, that it [nudity] is probably not good for children. But remember, that is a *psychological* [explanation] . . . of what we believe. . . . It may be true that children in nudist camps do not walk around with erections, but that only underscores the necessity . . . of this particular no-no: do not get sexually aroused inappropriately, even in a nudist camp.

This explanation of linking nudity to the *possibility* of inappropriate sexual arousal, which would be the danger from a religious perspective, was underlined as Father Corr explained the traditional Catholic perspective to us:

Social nudity, in public beaches for example, is not regulated for the Catholic by any particular church law, but it would be condemned under the concept of lewd conduct. It would be considered lewd because the body is considered sacred and parts of the body are sexually stimulating to observe. This also extends to familial nudity. In traditionally oriented Catholic families, a boy may be allowed to take a shower with his brother or a girl with her sister, but not boys and girls together.

It appears that most people we talked with connect nudity with sexuality or behavior leading to sexuality, not only those who hold a traditional religious point of view. Whether or not this is true (that is, whether the nude body is *inherently* sexually arousing or culturally taught and defined to be arousing) is not of primary importance for the issues in this book. What concerns us here is how people feel about the morality of familial and social nudity and how they communicate this moral value to their children. We are, of course, aware of the view

64

that the ban on familial nudity exists to reinforce the incest taboo. While we would accept the necessity of the incest taboo, we would question the allegation that familial and social nudity might represent threats to the incest taboo or to the general social controls on nonfamilial sexuality. As in so many other areas, more research needs to be done.

As Rabbi Kravitz alluded to, modern responses to familial nudity are often couched in terms of it not being good for the children (how much this really reflects the parents' discomfort rather than the child's well-being is not known). The belief that it is bad for children to see others naked appears to be traced back to Freud's writings suggesting that a young boy will compare the size of his penis to his father's and will feel woefully inadequate, thus causing problems in outgrowing the Oedipal phase. He may also fear losing his penis through castration as he imagines happened to his little sister. Freud also speculated that a girl will develop problems due to penis envy because she does not have what her brother and father have. Whether any of this is true or not or whether there is any harm or value to familial and social nudity we cannot answer here. There is precious little research on the subject.

Our focus here is on how the moral message is transmitted. On this matter a young woman said:

No one said anything about nudity. We just weren't permitted. My mother would walk around with at least her bra and underwear; my father could walk around in his boxer shorts; I could see my mother naked, my brothers could see my father naked, but I couldn't see my father in anything less than his boxer shorts, and my brothers never saw my mother in anything less than her bra and underwear. They never said it was wrong, but if my mother was in her bedroom and she wanted to change and my brother and I were sitting there, she would say to him: "Bobby, I want to change now, leave the room." She never explained why, but it was no big deal, so we accepted it.

Even today when I'm home for the summer from college, I may run from my room to the shower naked, and my mother

65

will say, if she sees me: "Daddy's here, he'll see you." And I'll
tell her: "I don't care, he's seen me before." She still seems to
get all upset by this but it's no big issue with me. At no time
when I was growing up did anyone ever tell me it was wrong
or a sin or immoral or anything negative about being nude in
front of my family or friends, it just wasn't done in my house.

I really have no idea of what the religious view of nudity is—
I suppose they are not too hyped up about it, but I don't really
know.

From a young male:

I never saw my parents or sister walk around naked. If I was
in my mother's room, she would go to the bathroom to get
dressed or she would wait until I walked out of the room. The
same with my father. I think I only saw him naked once when
we were on vacation and he walked out of a shower. The same
with my sister, I only saw her naked once when she came out
of the shower and the towel was not wrapped around her.

No one ever said it was wrong to be naked, but just that it
wasn't proper. "People don't do that." Nothing about the church
or God disapproving. I'm sure they believed that, but they never
communicated that to me.

And another young woman:

When my father gets dressed in the morning, he locks the door
to his bedroom. In no way did he ever let me in when he got
dressed. It was the same with my brother. If he ever came
downstairs in his underwear in the morning, my father would
get mad at him and yell at him to get dressed. We both have to
be completely dressed around our parents. It was always that
way.

The boys could get dressed in front of my father, and I could
get dressed in front of my mother, but if we are all together,
we have to be completely dressed. They never said that it had
anything to do with sex or morality but just that that was what
we had to do.

In spite of (or perhaps because of) these prohibitions in the home, children seem to enjoy experiencing nudity with each other—often as part of the games they play safely outside the purview of their parents. A young woman told us:

I used to play doctor with my sister who was a year older than me and this boy who lived in the house behind us. I was about 6 or 7 then. I was always afraid of being caught. We didn't really touch much, but mainly it was showing our parts to each other.

The playfulness might extend into the family, as another woman said:

My parents wouldn't walk into the family room nude, but they would walk from the bedroom to the bathroom without clothes on. If my brothers and I happened to see them or if I walked in on my mother naked, she wouldn't say anything or cover herself up, she just acted natural. I remember that my brothers would go from the bathroom to their bedrooms nude after a shower. I knew they would go by my room, so I would open it and say "Hi!" to try to embarrass them. My mother knew about it, but she never said anything about it.

These illustrations indicate a very puzzling value that is being communicated to people when they are young. Family nudity is not wrong, but it isn't right either. It appears that etiquette and a generalized social "other" is employed as the standard that is not attributable to the authority of religious morality or even a direct parental command. The abstract but at the same time ubiquitous "One doesn't do such things," was recalled to us by many people who remembered their parents giving this as the sole reason why young people shouldn't walk around nude. It is almost as if we had to create a new, albeit abstract, symbolic phrase legitimizing authority and morality: "One doesn't, people don't; therefore, we don't." But is this line of reasoning reasonable? The inquiring child asks: "Why not?"

and the well-considered but empty answer is a mere "Because!" A moral statement this certainly is not. The real issues, the fear of the breakdown of the incest taboo and the parents' own discomfort with the naked body, are avoided.

We do not mean to suggest that parents should or should not permit nudity in the home, and we have no quarrel with those who are concerned that a child or teenager may be sexually aroused by looking at a nude parent (it is also not uncommon for parents to be sexually attracted to their teenage children). Our point is that if parents wish all household members to be clothed appropriately in social situations, they should discuss their reasons so as to provide a basis for their decisions. The moral issue should be confronted, rather than sidestepped, and used as a means of helping to build the moral superstructure that the developing child needs. Let us again repeat the recurring theme of this book: If we want our children to have a strong moral underpinning to serve as a guideline for future decision making, they must have the experiences and the understanding at every stage of their young lives to be *capable* of making these moral decisions. Again, we stress that: *prohibition is not the same as morality.* Morality is positive, prohibition is negative. It is better to teach the values of telling the truth than the evils of lying.

Recently, Father Paul Dinter, a Newman Chaplain at Columbia University, conducted a study of eighty-nine young people who were identified with the church and campus ministry, involved in church life and knowledgeable about church doctrine and morals. In spite of their deep commitment, it appears that these young people rejected rules that appeared not to have reason behind them. Furthermore, Father Dinter indicated that simple appeals to vested authority alone are not very effective. He observed:

> The survey shows that we have not effectively linked spiritual growth and struggle with the normal process of growth and struggle that all men and women undergo in their lives. It is

68

not that these young people are unwilling to have norms or goals set for them, but rather that the goals seem remote from their experience.[5]

One of the few times that anyone mentioned attempts by the parents to deal with the morality of sexual behavior was this ironic story of a mother who took her children to church so they would learn moral norms:

> My father walked around nude and my mother frequently told him to cover up, but she never said anything to me. No one ever spoke about nudity or anything related to sexual morals at our church. You have to understand that this was a so-called liberal Congregationalist church. The minister was an understanding, kindly, genteel sort of person, and you just didn't talk about masturbation, nudity or things like that in front of him or in church activities. The irony is that my mother was really an agnostic and she took us there because she wanted me to get the "right" moral and ethical values. She believed in the moral and ethical teachings of Christ and wanted this taught to us, but they never talked about sexual morality there.

Other people we interviewed seem to be getting mixed messages from all sides:

> When my family travelled and knew there might be a choice of going to a nude beach or not, they would say: "We're very modest people and we couldn't do that." Or they would say to me: "If you expose yourself too much, then there is nothing to be desired for the boys to think about." If I really wanted to do it [remove my clothes at a nude beach], they probably would say: "Just don't do it around us."
> But as far as my religion goes [Armenian Orthodox], they have opened up much more over the years. I think that our religion wants to keep up with the times. I have this feeling

---

[5] Quoted in Basler, Howard. "A New Approach for Teaching Morality," *The Tablet* October 31, 1987, p. 24.

because as the Armenians moved from the Middle East to here, the church realized that they could no longer stick to their traditions that they had exercised back in the Middle Eastern countries.

Sometimes, whoever teaches sex standards in the family manages to communicate some very negative messages. These messages can remain in a child's mind for a long time. From a young woman:

In my family, being without clothes on was always wrong. We always had to cover up. It was considered shameful. We were told this by my mother. Since there were two girls and a boy in the house, I was not even allowed to walk out of my bedroom in a nightgown. I had to put a robe over the nightgown. I could walk around naked in front of my mother if I wanted to, but I had to be fully covered around my father or brother. I began to feel that what my mother considered shameful was our bodies. I hardly ever even looked at myself naked in the mirror because I hated my body in those days.

No one ever said that it was for religious reasons that we had to be covered, only that it was shameful to be without clothes if there was a boy or man around. I never heard anyone in the church or in religious school say that, only in my family. But, the parochial school teachers didn't say anything good about the body either.

And another young woman:

I would never be nude in front of my sisters or my sisters in front of me. I don't know if it's wrong now, but since my sisters are in their twenties, it's like looking at sexual bodies. If I had to undress in a gym, I hated it. I couldn't stand it even though it was only girls. I would hide behind the locker door or put my shirt on in such a way that I could change without anyone seeing me.

70

When we asked this young woman if she thought that boys were less likely to have the same problems in locker rooms and showers, she replied:

All boys have to do is wear their shorts underneath and then just take off their pants. But the guys don't take showers. In the school that I went to, the boys just put their tee shirts on after a basketball game because they hated the showers. I don't think they were worried about anybody grabbing them, or anything like that, it was just showing themselves in front of other boys.

The strong feelings some people have about nudity in front of their friends and locker room acquaintances seems related to (dare we say caused by?) the zealousness with which children, particularly girls, are protected from the eyes of males. A young woman from Puerto Rico told us:

When I was growing up, I could see my mother naked and my mother could see me naked, but my father wasn't permitted even to see me in my underwear. My mother wouldn't even allow him to see his granddaughters in their underwear. If a female grandchild at age two or three should lean back and expose her panties she would be told: "Cierre las piernas, que te ven los panties." ["Close your legs, your panties can be seen."]

If a young girl from about the age of two on was slow in getting dressed my mother had this saying: "Corre! Vistete! ⟨male name of someone in the house⟩ te va a ver las tetas." ["Hurry up and get dressed because ⟨male name⟩ is going to see your breasts."] My mother's friends would think it was a clever way of getting a kid dressed when they saw the girl getting very anxious.

My mother would be very careful to cover a baby's genitals not only from my father but from any male present if he was about 10 years old or older.

Think about it. What is the real message being communicated to these young people as they grow up in the house-

71

hold? "The naked body of someone of the opposite sex is so bad that something may happen to you if you look at it?" "Don't let your father see you naked because he may sexually attack you?" "I don't want you to see me naked because I have something to hide?" We are not suggesting that parents should not teach their children to remain clothed in social situations, but a simple "No!, because I say so," is not *teaching*, it is authoritarian prohibition. What is the moral message? Children seem to revel in being naked in warm weather and in the comfort of their home—without inhibition or embarrassment. Since these young children of two or three years of age cannot reason very well anyway, let them enjoy their nakedness when they are young. Then, when they are old enough to understand *teach* them what is and what is not appropriate and moral from your own religious and ethical perspective.

From childhood through the teen years, prohibition without appropriate reasons or moral values can result in a young person growing up with some doubt and shame about his or her body—especially after similar prohibitions that so often accompany childhood masturbation, as we suggested in the last chapter. Many of the scores of people we talked with recalled a sense of shame that accompanied the showing of their nude body, even in nonsexual situations. One of the few studies on this subject was conducted by Lou Lieberman in the late 1960s when he was on the faculty at the State University of New York at Albany. In a survey of over 250 students, he found that those young people who had casually seen both of their parents nude in the home (with no sexual overtones of course) were far more likely to feel comfortable with their bodies and to also feel satisfied with the size and shape of their genitalia and breasts. This may seem like trivial research to some, but is body self-image not a major aspect of self-esteem? Psychologist Judith Klein found that low self-esteem was frequently related not only to lack of strong ethnic ties but also to poor body image.[6] In the article about Father Dinter's research we mentioned earlier, Monsignor Howard Basler commented on this vital need for self-worth:

> Father Dinter proposes that we begin by refocusing our moral education to begin with a sense of self-worth. The early emphasis on sin and the disorder of concupiscence creates a negative bias clearly reflected in what the young people reject. The alternative is education designed to develop mature and chaste adults not just "keeping kids from genital activity until marriage."[7]

Bravo to Father Dinter and to Monsignor Basler! We need more voices to speak out to the community that parents, teachers and clergy must teach young persons *positive* images and feelings about themselves and their bodies and not constantly project images of a denying authority. In the lyrics of a popular song from the 1940s: "We must accentuate the positive, eliminate the negative, latch on to the affirmative and don't mess with Mister In-Between."

[6] Klein, Judith. *Jewish Identity and Self-Esteem*, New York: Institute on Pluralism and Group Identity of the American Jewish Committee, 1980.
[7] Basler, p. 24.

CHAPTER 5

Nonmarital Sex: Before and Instead of

When we first talked about the organization of this book, we planned to have separate chapters on premarital sex, cohabitation and choosing to have children outside of wedlock. We soon realized not only that the sexual moral issues were intertwined but also that the usual terms used to describe these behaviors were inadequate for the reality of life in the 1980s. For instance, a male friend of ours, who is 59 years old, has never married but has always maintained an active heterosexual sex life. Are we to say that he is still engaging in *pre*marital sex? Similarly, we know a divorced woman 39 years old (and holding)—should we consider her sexual activities *post*marital sex? If she thinks she might want to marry the man she is seeing, we might have to say that she is engaging in pre- and postmarital sex at the same time with the same man. Logical, but absurd. Labels and categories are sometimes useful when they help people organize their thinking, but like stereotypes they can sometimes become a trap and restrict thinking to the point where one cannot effectively deal with problems of the kind we raise in this book. Even if we decided to limit the popular term "premarital sex" to only younger people who have never been married, we would need a manual of definitions or the wisdom of Solomon to decide whether the age of 25 is the dividing line, or 35, or 40, or. . . . Similarly, we would have to decide if coital sexual intercourse is what we mean by "sex." Why not oral, manual, verbal, fantasy, etc.? Enough of such hairsplitting.

We have decided to take the easy way out and use some common sense. Sexual behavior means different things to different people, and the moral issues and rules concerning them vary by religion, denomination, community and minister. Therefore, we can only speak in the most general terms and let you fill in the details as to what specifically applies to your religious and ethical background, beliefs and commitments. The broad term that we will use is *nonmarital sex*, meaning acts (anything you consider to be sexual) between two consenting persons who are not married at the time; we will consider adultery in a later chapter. How should we define a situation in which one person is married and one isn't? As we will discuss in the adultery chapter, the traditional religious moral standards may even depend on whether it is the man or the woman who is married.

What is the background of the standards of nonmarital sexual morality we grapple with at the present time? Historians of antiquity believe that the biblical standards that emerged among the Hebrews had their roots among the people who lived in that area before the Hebrews. In the biblical Jewish tradition, virginity in a bride was always highly valued and the attitude toward sexual behavior outside the marital bed was strongly negative.[1] There were a number of reasons why nonmarital sex was probably uncommon. The ancient Hebrews married when they were very young, usually around the age of puberty and sometimes even earlier. Women were consid-

---

[1] Bullough, Vern L. *Sexual Variance in Society and History*, Chicago: University of Chicago Press, 1976, p. 59.

76

ered the property of their families, father and then husband. Having sex with any women other than your wife was considered in the same manner as taking someone's property without permission—stealing of a sort. The violator of these property rights had to make restitution. Among other peoples in the area, an adulterer was forced to give his wife to the father of the woman with whom he had had intercourse and then marry the daughter. If he was not married, he had to pay the father and marry the daughter, although the father could accept the payment but not give up the daughter in marriage.[2] Finally, according to Deuteronomy (22:14-21), if a man found that his wife was not a virgin at the time of marriage and the parents could not prove otherwise, the woman could be stoned.[3]

Early Christianity continued the essential Hebraic formulations of the relationship between sex and marriage. For example, St. Augustine and Christian theologians who followed held that intercourse had only one purpose and that was for procreation between husband and wife. Thus, sexual activity outside of marriage was condemned.[4]

By the early 1500s, reformers in the Catholic church were complaining, as did Martin Luther, that the times had become morally lax with unmarried women chasing men and offering themselves sexually. In taking a very dim view of this, Luther regarded fornication as a sin against the parents of the girl because, in effect, they lost a daughter due to the sexual acts of the girl.[5]

Having sex with a virgin, and other nonmarital sexual activity, gradually moved from the realm of being solely a religious issue to that of secular law. Under Edward IV, the English Parliament declared that a man who seduced a virgin who

---

[2] *Ibid.*, p. 52.
[3] Murstein, Bernard I. *Love, Sex, and Marriage Through the Ages*, New York: Springer, 1974, pp. 41–42.
[4] Bullough, p. 194.
[5] Murstein, pp. 195–196.

subsequently became pregnant had to marry her if she would have him; if not, he was compelled to give her one-third of his property or make some other arrangement to support the child. The Anglican church supported the growing view that sex outside of marriage was not only sinful but unlawful. At times, jail sentences were imposed for fornication, and even the death sentence could be declared (but rarely enforced) for adultery.

As in England, the colonies of the New World were more tolerant of nonmarital sex, or fornication, than of adultery. In all colonies except Rhode Island and Plymouth, although an adulterer could be put to death, punishment was usually limited to whippings, fines and branding.[6] If a child was born to a married couple before the "ordinary time," an indication of earlier fornication, the husband was usually only fined and his wife put into the stocks[7]—a humiliating public sentence, but more lenient than whipping or branding. In Plymouth Colony, the punishment for fornication was ten pounds or a whipping— still not as severe as for adultery. In the documents of the period, there is evidence to indicate that not only was there considerable nonmarital sex, but that engagement was considered as having social permission to have sex, as long as it didn't lead to children.[8,9]

We see then in early American history the beginning of a reversal of the trend that had developed for over a thousand years. Instead of religious morals and norms becoming the secular standards, contemporary social sexual behavior patterns coexisted with religious norms even when they were in moral conflict. We believe that this trend of secular norms becoming dominant over religious norms in the area of sexuality has reached a peak in the present generation in which we are

---

6 *Ibid.*, p. 318.
7 *Ibid.*, p. 319.
8 *Ibid.*
9 For another excellent account of this period, see Bell, Robert B. *Premarital Sex in a Changing Society*, Englewood Cliffs, N.J.: Prentice-Hall, 1966, Chapter 1.

witnessing the mainstream religions grappling with how to adapt their sexual moral norms to fit today's secular norms. We will discuss this in more detail later in this chapter.

Although attitudes began to change even in colonial times, the "big shift" from a religious to a secular basis for sexual morality, particularly by the younger generations, seems to have begun in the late nineteenth century. What happened? In order to understand this, we have to realize that the traditional sexual moral code of limiting sexual activity to the marital bond was strengthened by two very real possibilities: first, that the sexual act could result in a pregnancy, and second, that the sexual act could result in contracting venereal disease. Couple these fears with a belief (remember, this is long before the days of Freud and the recognition that we all have libidinal impulses) that the female was the sexually passive and sexually uninterested half of the species who could only be "awoken" by a male, and we have a powerful means of social control of at least female sexuality, if not male. (These factors, along with traditional religious interpretations of the relationship between males and females, contributed to the male-female double standard we will discuss later.)

Although attitudes concerning female sexuality were changing through the early twentieth century, even as late as the 1950s when Kinsey and his associates conducted their research, this control over female sexuality through denial of female interest in sex was still a widespread attitude:

Some 45 percent of the females in the sample recognized that their lack of sexual responsiveness had been a factor in limiting their premarital activity . . . but it seems clear that a lack of responsiveness or an inability to respond was even more important than the females themselves understood. As someone long ago recognized, it is easier to abstain from sin when one is not physically or physiologically endowed with the capacity—or with much capacity—to sin.

Fear of pregnancy ranked next, with 44 percent of the females

79

considering that this had been one of the factors which had
limited their premarital coitus.[10]

Going back to the "big shift" in the late nineteenth century,
1876 was a milestone year in the history of sexual attitudes
and behavior. The first vulcanized rubber condom generated
a great deal of interest when it was displayed at the 1876
Philadelphia World's Fair. Sociologist Ira L. Reiss thinks that
the sexual liberation of women, especially in the middle and
upper classes, was due primarily to the vulcanized rubber
condom, the pessary cap and the diaphragm, all developed in
the late nineteenth century. He goes on to note that dating
with chaperones present was all but gone and young couples
had more opportunity to be alone for longer periods.[11] (This
social dating pattern was greatly accelerated by the invention
of the automobile, which ensured even more privacy for a
couple to go off alone.)

The development of an effective oral contraceptive in the
1960s as well as the common use of antibiotics and other
medications for the easy treatment of venereal disease all but
eliminated the two fears associated with nonmarital sex. (This
was before the AIDS epidemic for which there is no cure at
this time.) The elimination of these two fears contributed
significantly to the greater sexual liberation of the 1960s and
1970s. Moral controls and taboos (especially over female sexuality) still remained. The difference was (and still is) that the
bases of these controls had shifted away from the religious
beliefs to more contemporary social ones. According to Kinsey
and his associates:

[10] Kinsey, Alfred C., W. Pomeroy, C. Martin and P. Gebhard. *Sexual Behavior in the
Human Female*, Philadelphia: W. B. Saunders, 1953. Reprinted in *The Family And the
Sexual Revolution*, edited by Edwin M. Schur. Bloomington, Ind.: Indiana University
Press, 1964, p. 23.
[11] Reiss, Ira L. "Changing Sociosexual Mores," in *Handbook of Sexology*, edited by
J. Money and H. Musaph. New York: Excerpta Medica, 1977, p. 313.

In their own analyses of the factors which had restricted their premarital coitus, 89 percent of the females in the sample said that moral considerations had been of primary importance. . . . However, some of them insisted that they were not accepting the traditional codes just because they were the codes, and believed that they had developed their attitudes as a result of their own rational analyses of what they considered to be expedient, decent, respectable, fine, sensible, right or wrong, better or best. This represented an interesting attempt on the part of the younger generation to proclaim its emancipation from the religious tradition, but most of them were still following the traditions without having found new bases for defending them.[12]

What is interesting here is that the sexual standards had not changed much, just the justification or moral bases for them. Perhaps this is an important lesson for today: It is not that people want to eliminate sexual moral codes, on the contrary, we believe that most people hunger for them. But, what is still rejected is the authoritarian bases for the standards. It perhaps becomes a major challenge to theologians and religious educators and even to parents to fit sexual standards into a moral system that makes sense rather than merely proclaiming an authoritarian, "You don't do this because I tell you not to," or evoking some aspect of fear as a moral basis. We are not suggesting that we have the answer, but answers will not come unless we can accept the legitimacy of the *questioning* of the traditional moral bases.

If you grew up in this country or elsewhere in Western society before the 1960s, you very likely believed that there was basically only one traditional, that is religious, moral standard regarding nonmarital sex and that it was a very restrictive one. Very likely, most people still believe that religion and nonmarital sex are contradictory. We suspect that most

---

[12] Kinsey *et al.*, p. 23.

people believe that this standard was set forth in the Bible and continues to the present in traditional Judaism and Christianity. Although various sects and groups within particular religions take somewhat different positions and emphases, most people probably believe that this classic statement by Pope Pius XI in 1930 represents *the* traditional Judeo-Christian moral standard:

> Since the duty entrusted to parents for the good of their children is of such high dignity and of such great importance, every use of the faculty given by God for the procreation of new life is the right and privilege of the married state alone, by the law of God and of nature, and must be confined absolutely within the sacred limits of that state.[13]

Let us see what Rabbi Kravitz says about the biblical sources of our nonmarital moral standards. (In this book, we repeatedly present Rabbi Kravitz's interpretations before Father Corr's, not because we love Father Corr less—in fact they are both very good friends of ours—but since Christianity emerged from Judaism, many of the former's tenets can only be understood in the context of Old Testament teaching.)

> Traditionally, premarital sex was not acceptable, but the prohibition did not apply equally to men and women. Virginity was prized in women. If we take the Biblical period as an example, we read (Deut. 22:13ff) of a man complaining that his wife was not a virgin when he married her. The parents of the bride bring the sheet upon which the first act of intercourse occurred to prove that she was. The complainant is fined and the proceeds go to the father. If, however, the complaint is established, and the bride was not a virgin, then, according to the Biblical text, the girl is stoned. Rabbinic Judaism modified the law so that the complaint could not be made and the girl could not be stoned, but still the stress upon virginity for women is apparent.

---

[13] Pope Pius XI, *Casti Connubii*, 1930. Quoted in *Sex Isn't That Simple: The New Sexuality on Campus*, by Richard Hettlinger. New York: Seabury Press, 1974, p. 48.

We find no comparable Biblical punishment for the loss of virginity in the male.

One has the feeling that part of the issue of virginity is that of contractual status, that a virgin was promised and there was a question of whether a virgin was produced. It is noteworthy that the complaining husband is not punished by more than a fine should his complaint not be established.

As the centuries went by, on-going tradition would interpret the Biblical passages in moral terms. These new/old interpretations would then be projected back into the Biblical text, though it might be argued that the situations from whence they arose themselves arose from contractual situations.

Today, the Reform and Conservative movements might be said to be doing much the same thing, as they apply contemporary ethical understandings to certain Biblical passages. The Orthodox movements might be said to move a bit slower as they apply rabbinic and medieval understandings to the Biblical text. The tendency of all movements is to claim that they are following what the Torah (and the rest of the Biblical texts) "really" means.

Rabbi Kravitz goes on to comment about attempts at a more modern sexual ethic that reflects contemporary attitudes toward nonmarital sex:

This is not easy to do since once we move away from the contractual obligations as a means of control over premarital sex and toward individual centered control, we have problems. To build a sexual ethic around "having a meaningful, loving, caring relationship" opens the door to someone saying to himself or herself, perhaps without realizing it: "Since I want to have sex, I am now in a meaningful, loving, caring relationship," until the sexual desires are no longer there or something else goes wrong and so the relationship ends. We have not yet been able to formulate a new religious sexual ethic which seems to work.

Of course, from an Orthodox and traditional point of view, it is not only that the purpose of sex is to be able to have children, but the current notion of a woman wanting to have a child even though she is not married is wholly unacceptable. Traditionally, one does not have the freedom of choice to have children outside of marriage, or to choose not to have children when one is married.

Not surprisingly, redefining sexual ethics in the modern world is a problem facing many in the Roman Catholic church. Says Father Finbarr Corr:

Until the 1960s, the principles of sexual morality and ethics were very clear. There were church laws which the people interpreted as if they were black and white: If you obeyed the law, you didn't sin; if you disobeyed the law, you sinned. It was pretty specific: If you were unmarried, you could not masturbate, you could not touch a girl's breast or vagina, obviously, you could not have intercourse, you couldn't even engage in prolonged kissing since the intent was sexual pleasure.

Now with the Second Vatican Council, the same standard was presented except that the church placed a greater emphasis upon the dignity of the person with respect to the law; priests had a greater latitude in determining whether an act was sinful or not. Sometimes this has resulted in priests taking a position which is different from the religious law due to different interpretations of what it means to act on the basis of conscience.

Most Catholics today are pretty clear on the church's position concerning abortion and homosexual acts, but it is in the other areas that they often have difficulty in determining whether their sexual behavior would be considered a sin or not. For example, sexual intercourse by a young unmarried person is still considered sinful, but if in the course of expressing affection for each other they should get sexually aroused, this would not necessarily be a sin, unless they deliberately continue their behavior once they are aware that they are aroused. Again, as we said earlier, intention is a very important consideration.

Some people have said that the church has an antisex attitude. To understand the roots of why this attitude appears to be there, we have to look at the long history of the church and male attitudes in general. There was a time when males were considered superior to women. Women were not supposed to have any interest in sex. It was understood that men did but, presumably, they went to prostitutes. Women were supposed to be pure, it was O.K. for men to be slightly off, but women had to go to the altar with a white dress. I have heard young Catholic men bragging about their sex lives with young women when they were engaged. However, it was not the fiancée who they had sex with, but other women. They still want their fiancées to be virgins when they go to the altar and will abstain from any sex with them.

The kinds of changes that have taken place in contemporary Roman Catholic guidelines for moral sexual behavior are not always easy to explain to lay persons or young people. In contrast, the older legalistic approach of clearly defining right and wrong in sexual matters had the advantage of simplicity, if not flexibility. But, as Father Corr stated, emphasis shifted after the Second Vatican Council, and although some Catholic theologians may not have completely embraced the Council's directions, others have. This has precipitated a debate that is still going on.[14]

Of all the issues we examine in this book, the question of whether or not to engage in some form of sexual activity before, instead of or after marriage is the most complex one in terms of moral standards. This is due to the very confusing set of sexual standards that has developed as part of the culture of the people instead of as a moral code that emanates from religion. For example, there are unmarried young women we know of who believe it is O.K. to have coital sex with someone they love but not with someone they do not love. There are others who believe that they can honestly present themselves as virgins to a prospective mate if they are "technical virgins," that is, they may have had all kinds of oral, anal and manual sex, sometimes with many partners, but without vaginal penetration.

---

[14] Nelson, James B. *Between Two Gardens: Reflections on Sexuality and Religious Experience.* New York: Pilgrim Press, 1983, p. 60.

There are a range of possible standards confronting both young and old people today. These standards do not apply only to possible choices one has in dating relationships, from the first date on through engagement. One, the "double standard," may even carry on into the relationship between husbands and wives, where cultural norms are more tolerant of male adultery than for the wives. We will discuss this in Chapter 7.

Ira Reiss developed a list of sexual standards over twenty years ago. Even today, these standards still represent the choices that face unmarried people (although we again stress that the double standard also applies to married couples in many groups):

1. *Abstinence*—Premarital intercourse is considered wrong for both sexes.
   a. Petting without affection—Petting is acceptable even when affection is negligible.
   b. Petting with affection—Petting is acceptable only in a stable, affectionate relationship.
   c. Kissing without affection—Only kissing is acceptable, but no affection is required.
   d. Kissing with affection—Only kissing is acceptable, and only in a stable, affectionate relationship.
2. *Double standard*—Males are considered to have greater rights to premarital intercourse.
   2. Orthodox—Males may have intercourse, but females who do so are condemned.
   b. Transitional—Males have greater access to coitus, but females who are in love or engaged are allowed to have intercourse.
3. *Permissiveness without affection*—Premarital intercourse is right for both sexes regardless of the amount of affection present.
   a. Orgiastic—Pleasure is of such importance that precautions are not stressed.

86

b. Sophisticated—Pleasure is stressed, but precautions to avoid VD and pregnancy are of first importance.
4. *Permissiveness with affection*—Premarital intercourse is acceptable for both sexes if part of a stable, affectionate relationship.
   a. Love—Love or engagement is a prerequisite for coitus.
   b. Strong affection—Strong affection is a sufficient prerequisite for coitus.[15]

We present these standards in their entirety because we believe that they have more than mere academic applicability today. We do not espouse one or another of these standards— that is for the reader to choose based upon his or her religious and ethical beliefs. We would like you to think about which standard(s) you were taught as a child (or which one(s) you teach your children, if you are a parent) and which one(s) you now accept for yourself. Do you follow the same standard(s) that you preach to others? If not, do you really understand why you have chosen different standards? And, which one(s) should you teach your children? Do they fit into a consistent moral code that makes sense? Let us now see what these standards mean and how they may be used.

Officially, at least traditionally, abstinence would probably be considered by most people to be the religious moral standard for nonmarital sex. However, even here, we have noted some variation between the different religious groups as they attempt to adhere to this standard today, as well as variation among different ministers, priests and rabbis within the same religious group. And, of course, this is reflected in the positions of the parents who follow these religions. Some will say that kissing is acceptable only when there is affection, while others will condone even casual petting as part of the "rehearsal" for the sexual marital role. Of course, there are some religions that

[15] Adapted from Reiss, Ira L. *Premarital Sexual Standards in America*, New York: Free Press, 1960, p. 251. Quoted in *The Social Context of Premarital Sexual Permissiveness*, by Ira L. Reiss. New York: Holt, Rinehart, and Winston, 1967, p. 19.

87

will not even permit this because of the belief that it places some young persons at a risk of losing control and going much further.

As for the infamous "double standard," despite the women's movement and male consciousness-raising groups, letters and calls that come to *Dr. Ruth* as well as many of the people we have interviewed say that the "orthodox" double standard still lingers on and still reflects female as well as male thinking. Many mothers and fathers we know (no names, please) who are otherwise very liberal, insightful and well educated show little or no concern about their teenage sons having sex but certainly watch their daughters like the proverbial hawks. These are the same parents who marched triumphantly through the various liberation movements of the 1960s and even considered themselves sexually liberated. We know that from biblical days to the present the double standard was probably implicit (and sometimes explicit) even in religious laws and rules, but that doesn't make it fair or moral. It may be true that some parents rationalize this by thinking that it is their daughter who could become pregnant not their son, but their son could make someone else's daughter pregnant. ("Well, my son could use a condom." "But, Mom, your daughter could also use a contraceptive."—Be fair!) A clear and typical story of parental values reflecting the double standard was told to us by this young woman:

Was the attitude toward my brother different? It sure was, even up to last Christmas when I visited my family. I was sitting there with my sister Maryann, who was 19 years old, and my mom and dad, who were eating dinner. Maryann's twin brother Paul had left in the afternoon to go to his girlfriend's apartment for the weekend. She lived alone in the apartment. Maryann wanted to stay out late that night, but my father said that she had to be home by midnight. My sister said: "Dad, Paul left and went to his girlfriend's house and I can't even stay out late?" He said: "No, you have to be home by midnight." "But, Dad . . ." "I don't care, Paul's a boy, you're a girl. You are to be home by midnight, and if you don't like it, what can I say? You get home by midnight. When you are in my house you do as I say."

What do you think that such a moral standard does for the self-esteem of an adolescent girl or young woman? Can we ever teach moral principles and standards when we devalue the worth of a person because of her sex or for any other demeaning reason? Or can we base moral teaching only on personal authority? We think not. As we have said before, and will continue to say throughout this book, a moral code must be consistent, fair, known and integrated into all parts of life. If a young woman cannot be trusted after the witching hour of midnight, she is being told that she is not trusted at 9:00 P.M. as well. If the parents are worried to the point of not being able to sleep after midnight, then they are worried before midnight as well. If it is fear of the unknown because they don't know the location of their son or daughter after midnight, they should also worry before midnight. These are issues of concern, common sense and courtesy between parents and their children. Parents do worry, as both of us have, when their children are out; some of it is natural (due to separation anxiety) and some unreasonable. Children should be made to understand this and let their parents know where they can be reached in an emergency. But these are common sense and courtesy issues to be discussed and agreed upon by all concerned, they are not issues of sexual morality and certainly should not be the basis for teaching a moral double standard. Parents need to separate moral principles from authoritarianism. If children only learn moral principles as a function of authoritarian rules, they become like a heavy yoke, to be lifted as soon as they are out of sight of the parents.

What does Professor Reiss mean by "permissiveness without affection"? Although this has not been very widespread as a sexual standard, in our society, it certainly became an issue among some during the 1960s and 1970s as a reaction to the double standard. From a moral perspective, it appears to negate any moral principle because it removes all elements of rules for social control and self-control that are in the best interest of the individual and society. One would have to say that it is completely hedonistic in that the primary goal of the sexual act is self-gratification and not related to the other person. Although few people would admit that they hold to this standard, tragically, it is probably responsible for many of the teenage pregnancies today. That is, we would suggest that when people, young and old, have not really accepted (or perhaps were never taught?) a moral code for sexual behavior, their natural biological urges may impel them to have sex when they shouldn't. Teaching them that abstinence is an option is not the same as teaching a moral principle. If we teach that abstinence is an option, logically nonabstinence becomes another option. We can't talk about one without the other. If we accept nonabstinence as an option, we must expect that many will adopt "permissiveness without affection" as a standard—many already have. We do not wish to suggest however that if abstinence alone is taught as a moral principle, nonabstinence will not be considered and chosen—of course it will. It is a reality of life we cannot pretend will go away if we simply do not talk about it.

And finally, "permissiveness with affection": Just as abstinence was clearly the stated moral sexual norm in the past, and still is for many religious groups that we tend to describe as "traditional" or "orthodox" or "fundamentalist," discussions among many people concerned with sexual morals and values indicate that "permissiveness with affection" is possibly becoming the new "acceptable" sexual morality. These discussions are taking place both inside and outside the religious establishments in this country and abroad in all the mainstream religions that are trying to come to grips with what has appeared to be a growing gulf between traditional religious teachings and the reality of the modern world. The hope is that where other standards cannot be integrated with and supportive of a system of sexual morals and values consistent with other moral principles of religion, these can be. We believe this to be an exciting and encouraging movement within religion that will strengthen, not weaken, morality as the guideline for helping people make the correct choices in sexual situations.

Taking one last look at Reiss's standards, we see that, short of total abstinence for all persons, the standards and morals that are taught and that young people may choose often involve the risk of pregnancy. Therefore, although sex education is not the point of this book, we must strongly urge that those who follow these standards also follow suitable contraceptive precautions in order to minimize the chances of unwanted pregnancies. It follows that those who accept the standard of "permissiveness without affection," should at least follow what Reiss calls the "sophisticated" subtype (using contraceptives) rather than the "orgiastic," which throws all caution to the wind. Finally, those spokespersons in the community who favor the teaching of abstinence must also strongly advocate the use of contraceptives by those who do not accept abstinence as a moral standard. An unwillingness to acknowledge the necessity for these people to use contraceptives would indicate an insensitivity to the sufferings of all who do not share their moral belief.

Let us turn now to some of the men and women we interviewed. Who taught them about moral issues and standards regarding nonmarital sex? An interesting response to our questions from a young woman showed the interplay between religious identification and secular sex standards:

> I never heard anything from the synagogue or any other Jewish religious source about the necessity to remain a virgin until I got married, but the message was communicated to me by my mother in a very indirect way. I know that my mother was a virgin when she got married at the age of 20. She will freely admit now that she probably got married at that young age because she was so frustrated. She believed then that all the

good girls were virgins and all the bad girls were not. Of course, all the good girls were the Jewish girls and all the bad girls were the Italian girls in the neighborhood. In that sense I grew up believing, from my earliest days, that good Jewish girls did not have premarital sex. It had nothing to do with religion, it was from a social perspective.

I remember, on one occasion, I heard a sermon about the corruption of the Jewish family, many years ago. The rabbi said something about Jews living together who were not married. But my family never said anything about it from a religious point of view. They did say that they didn't think that living together was a good idea, not because it was immoral, but that it's important to have your own space when you are not married.

And another young woman told of this innovative way in which her mother helped to keep her a virgin:

When I was 13 or 14, I had a best friend who was very sexually active. She had a boyfriend at all times and she told me enough details to fill many books. I don't know whether or not she used contraceptives, but she did talk about sex a lot. I thought it was disgusting because at that age I had barely kissed a boy. I was extremely envious because I didn't think that I was attractive enough to get a boyfriend. But my mother used to say to me: "Kathleen, the type of man who's going to appreciate you is going to be older. The boys you meet now are just boys and they can't appreciate you, so wait till you get to college. When you get older, they will realize what a good girl you are." What she meant was that the reason young girls had boyfriends was that they were "fooling around" and having sex with them, but that when I got older, the ones I would want and who would want to be with me wouldn't just look for that. They would look for other things. She said that many times. We never really talked about sex, but once when we were talking about my going to college, she said that she thought a girl today should be a virgin. When I asked her about the guy, she said: "No, he's going to need to know what to do." She shocked me because

92

she was the daughter of a minister and had always been so religious.

My father never really said that I should or should not be a virgin except when I was leaving for college. Then he sat me down and said, in effect: "I'll love you no matter what happens. Whatever you do you can always tell me and I'll still love you."

It seemed to be all right for me to kiss and pet with boys, although my mother never was clear about what I could or could not do. I came home with a hickey on my neck once but she only made fun of it—she didn't punish me. She probably would draw the line at oral sex because I guess she would consider that to be too intimate and that the guy wouldn't respect me. That was important to her; to have the boys respect me.

And one more young woman:

My mother never said specifically that my body wasn't mine, the way I had been taught in parochial school, but she made it very clear to me that sex was forbidden until I was married and that if I did engage in sex, I would be a slut or a very loose woman. Even kissing—she knew that I kissed boys when I grew up, but I don't think that she even approved of that. We never really had any discussion about sex, but she was always telling me that it was wrong.

Yet another young woman described her father's restrictive approach:

I don't remember my mother ever telling me that premarital sex was wrong, but I do remember some messages that my father gave me. I remember being told that I couldn't go to my fifth grade dance because "good" girls didn't go to dances like that. He said: "If you go to dances like that you will get a bad reputation."

I was allowed to go to my third and fourth grade dances, but when I got to the fifth and sixth grades, I wasn't allowed to go. When I asked him about all the other kids in the neighborhood

93

that went, he said: "I don't care what the rest of the kids do, you're a good girl, and you are not going to go to that dance." I argued with him: "I'm a good girl, I'm not going to do anything." He never told me what he meant by a "good girl" but somehow I knew. "Bad" girls were the ones who sat in the corner and "made out" with boys. I didn't really know what that meant but only that it was wrong.

In the sixth, seventh and eighth grade, I was told: "You are daddy's girl and you won't want to date boys until you are 16."

These four quotations illustrate a very important theme that is present in Western culture and that we believe to be counterproductive and even destructive to a young woman's self-image and the way in which young men see women. This is the "madonna and whore complex"—or sometimes more informally called the "good girl–bad girl complex." Recall Father Corr's young men, even some who held traditional religious values, who actively pursued women to have sex with but wanted their wives to be virgins. Since the abstinence before marriage standard has been the traditional one in the Jewish and Christian heritages, and despite current debates is still the one most people seem to believe is attached to this heritage, telling a young woman that "good girls" don't do this is a message to encourage boys to test girls to see if they are "good." It perpetuates the insidious double standard because we have no comparable "saint and satyr complex"—or "good boy–bad boy complex"—regarding sexuality. A recent discussion on the Phil Donahue show concerned a 14-year-old boy who had been seduced by his 37-year-old female teacher. At the beginning of the show, no one seemed to think that the woman should have gone to jail for this, but as Phil pointed out, if it had been a 37-year-old male teacher and a 14-year-old girl, everybody would have been outraged. This double standard grows out of the mixed moral messages—even to the point of hypocrisy— that some otherwise well-intentioned parents pass on to their children. They are well intentioned, but misguided.

The concept of what a good girl does, which is different from what a boy does, is not a moral message, and as the child gets older, it will become clear that there are "good" girls who do have sex and "bad" girls who do not. Serious problems of self-image may develop if a girl believes that she is now "bad" or a "whore" because she experimented with sex—she might as well keep on engaging in sex because she cannot undo the label. This is not morality; it is ineffectual parental pressure. If a young girl (or a young boy) commits an immoral act, *she* is not immoral, the *act* is immoral, and she can still be a worthy person. But if the act becomes a label for the person, can she still feel as worthy and try to live up to high ideals? Sociologists call this "labelling," and much research has pointed to the high likelihood that negative labelling will cause a child to increasingly live up to the label. If "friends" pick up on the label, they too will treat the child as if the label were true. A father who calls his daughter a "whore" because he finds out that she has had sex may be pushing his daughter to engage in even more sex—after all, what has she to lose once she is labelled?

Sometimes the moral message is couched in terms that make it difficult for a young person to place it in the context of a moral system. Virginity as a value becomes so isolated from the rest of sexual morality that it may become an end in itself. A young woman from one of the Caribbean islands told us:

In my family background, we really didn't talk about whether it is right or wrong to have premarital sex. Everything seemed to be related to the wedding ceremony. My mother says that it is beautiful to have the white dress in church and that if someone could have that it is a really beautiful thing. To be able to wear the white veil in church, to her that's really important. I agree that it's nice to have the white dress, to be able to wear the white dress and the veil and go down the aisle as a virgin. And if you can do it, that's the way to go, but if you can't, it's no big deal.

I don't know if I think this way [remain a virgin in order to wear white] because the ceremony is beautiful, or if it's because

95

the church says it should be that way, or if you are really proving your love by being with only one person. I was never taught any religious reasons for remaining a virgin, only that no man would want you if you weren't. All the church said was that you had to wear the white dress and veil and you couldn't pretend by wearing white if you were not a virgin because God would know and you have sinned by lying to God. The fear of every girl from the islands is that God would punish her for lying by making her veil fall off in front of everybody.

No, I never went to a wedding where the girl didn't wear white, even those who had had sex. Some of them didn't wear a white veil because the father has to lift the veil, and he would know when he looked into his daughter's eyes that she wasn't a virgin. So to be on the safe side, a girl would say that she didn't want to wear a veil.

Is this a moral message that was communicated by the parents? We would have to say no. Even though the outcome of control (abstinence) might have been what the parents and the religion desired, the method for producing that result rested upon a value, wearing a white dress, not upon basic moral principles. As such, the value of retaining one's virginity appears to be based on wearing white in church rather than on some inherent worth of the principle of chastity outside of marriage. It appears that wearing white is a community standard rather than any moral standard. Since community standards may rapidly change, and morality is supposed to be of a higher order of consideration and far more basic to our lives, we would prefer that her values emerge or are selected *because* of her moral code rather than being dictated by "what the neighbors think."

Another, perhaps odd, way of confronting the issue of the morality of nonmarital sexual behavior can best be described by the term *denial*. This from a 21-year-old woman:

This year was the first year I ever heard my mom talk about premarital sex being sinful. She said it was a sin, and I said:

96

"Why is it a sin?" All she said was: "The Bible says that you shouldn't do it." I said: "What are you talking about? Where does it say that in the Bible?" And, she couldn't tell me.

One day my mother was going through my older sister's dresser drawers and she found a diaphragm. She was very upset, but my sister told her that it was her friend's, and my mother believed her. I'm sure that my mother just didn't want to believe that she was having sex. My mom didn't tell my dad about it because he would have died.

My sister, who is dating someone in a long-distance relationship, has to go out of town to see him. My mom would ask her: "Where do you sleep when you visit him?" And she would say: "Oh, I sleep in his roommate's room." My mom would believe her. It not only would hurt her if she was told the truth, but I really don't think she wants to know and deal with it. She would think she had done something wrong in bringing us up, so I don't tell her anything. I feel bad about lying to her, that is immoral, but she would be so upset if she knew that we just don't tell her anything. We don't talk much about any of the boys I go out with, just everyday conversation. I get more involved with discussions with my sister. I really don't think my mom wants to know. She asks questions like: "Who do you like?" and "Where do you go?" and things like that, but she never asks what I do. She would never ask me anything more about sex except: "Did he kiss you?" because she wouldn't dream that I'd do anything else.

Sometimes confused messages come from the sources we would least expect. A young male:

You could see during the junior and senior years [in parochial school] that we were having more and more difficulty with what we were being taught [about sex and morals] that we had to repeat like a parrot compared with what our minds were telling us. You could see the pull, you could really see the pull, and that was one of the big disputes that I had with Catholic schooling because they didn't allow you to think. They kept telling us to think—in biology class, in chemistry class, in history and En-

97

glish—they would say: "Think, think, think." But when it came
to religion where we discussed morality, it became: "Don't think."
I could see this pull among my friends, when they would say:
"That's bull! You tell me to question everything else, not this."
What happened was that the [differences between the] sexual
reality of what happened outside the classroom and what we
were taught about sexual morals got wider and wider.

The brothers knew what was going on, and while they were
in class, they taught what they were told to teach, but when you
got to know some of them after you were in the school two or
three years, it was "Brother Robert" while you were in class and
"Hi, Bob, what's going on?" on the outside. In many ways,
because they were young, they identified more with us than
with the structure of the priesthood they were going to join.
Also, they hadn't taken the vows of celibacy yet so they thought
differently. When they took their collars off, we all looked the
same. We knew they chased the girls too, not all of the brothers,
just some.

Paradoxically, the most common form of communication
about sex standards and values often occurs through silence.
This was described to us by a young woman:

The moral things that were emphasized in the church and in
Bible classes were: loving other people, feeling responsibility
toward other people, never stealing, being an honest person
and things like that. As far as sexuality, I don't remember ever
getting any teaching about it, except that marriage was looked
upon as good. They never explained adultery or fornication. I
think that's because they didn't get into the catechism kind of
teaching as in the Catholic church. Liberal Protestant churches
don't get into that. We would tell Bible stories, and things like
that. The things I remember being taught were that Jesus loves
the little children of the world and discussions of a big picture
of Jesus with Indians and blacks and others—a united nations
kind of picture. That's what I remember being emphasized.

No, when we heard Bible stories, even about Sodom and
Gomorrah or Noah or the rest, no one ever spoke about the

98

sexual connotations in these stories. Remember, WASPs [white Anglo-Saxon Protestants] don't like to talk about sex at all. They just don't like to mention it. It's really true! The way that they tell you that it's not allowed is by the big silence. It's like the big lie, that it just doesn't exist.

Sexual morals are expected to be taught by the parents, but a lot of parents just shove it under the rug. No one in the church teaches the parents about sexuality or sexual morals, and no one asks how the parents are supposed to learn because everyone is just too embarrassed to talk about it.

A young woman who told us that her mother never talked to her about premarital sex also told us this story:

When I was a senior in high school, my best friend was a freshman who was living in a dorm at college in another city. Before she left for college, she and her parents came over to my parents' house. Knowing how my parents felt about my sleeping away from home, I manipulated the situation and asked my mother and father in front of her mother and father if I could visit her and stay in her dormitory room after the semester began. My parents couldn't say no in front of her parents without saying: "No, we don't trust you girls," in front of them. So they said O.K.

When the semester began, I asked my parents if I could go stay with her for a weekend. They gave me a hard time but I reminded them that they had agreed. They let me go—I went about three or four times. Every time I went—I would leave on a Friday—my mother would begin to get mad at me the Monday before. She would hardly talk to me all week, be cold and abrupt, and very stern. Then when I got back, she would be mad for three or four more days and then begin to loosen up until she got back to normal.

I couldn't understand this until about three or four years later, until I moved to Florida and came back for a visit. We were at a family picnic and all drinking and my mother was a little tipsy and out it came why she got mad at me. She was mad at me because she didn't know if I was going to sleep with someone and get pregnant. Rather than talk about it, she would just get mad at me.

Here is a mother who believed it was best to remain a virgin until marriage. Even though she was concerned and worried about her daughter, she made very little effort to talk with the young girl as she grew up. Instead of confronting the issue, she avoided it.

The strict rules, warnings and silence parents cling to instead of, and in order to avoid, discussing the morality, ethics and values of nonmarital sex help to bring about the very situations they fear most. Rather than providing a solid moral foundation for their sexual standards, parents impose meaningless rules or avoid the topic altogether. As a result, most children have no moral basis or understanding for their sexual activities—so they experiment, they wonder, they defy, and (too often) they get pregnant.

Denial—anger—hypocrisy—double standard—authoritarianism—folk myths—silence—antifemale stereotyping—and yet all too often parents wonder aloud to their friends; social commentators on TV ask; politicians want answers to: "Why are so many young people acting in a sexually immoral manner?" We ask them: "Don't you know?"

CHAPTER 6

A Theoretical Interlude

Why a "theoretical interlude"? Our publisher, Harcourt Brace Jovanovich is blessed with terrific editors. We had originally placed this material in the chapter on nonmarital sex, but they pointed out that too much theoretical discussion in that chapter was confusing and that much of what we had to say really concerned *all* the issues raised in the book. We agreed, so before going on with the other areas, we would like to go more deeply into some of the points raised in previous chapters as well as help provide a framework for some of the issues that we will raise in the following chapters.

If this brief chapter had a subtitle, it would probably be "The Changing Morality of Religion." In this interlude, we will focus on the conflict between traditional religious morality and modern society and lifestyles. We will see how many religions are changing their strict "legalistic" standards to adjust to the complexities and implications of modern industrial societies and current times and how these changes are both liberating and confusing. We will stress how parents, schools and religions must adapt both the style and content of their teaching so that these changes are understandable rather than bewildering. Only if they can be understood can they serve as a basis for moral decision making. Our discussion will look at what some theologians and religious scholars have to say about these issues, and we will offer our own perspective and insights.

As we noted in the last chapter, the Second Vatican Council opened a debate on sexual morality, as well as other aspects of morality, that continues to the present day. Similar discussion and re-examination of moral standards is also taking place in many other religious groups.

Theology professor James B. Nelson says that the book that was most influential in stimulating this debate for Catholics was *Human Sexuality: New Directions in American Catholic Thought*.[1] Nelson summarizes its interpretation of the council's emerging philosophy on sexual morality as follows:

> Now the focus is unequivocally on the person and his or her "creative growth toward integration." . . . Seven values are singled out as particularly significant, characterizing actions that promote such growth and integration: the sexual expression will be self-liberating, other-enriching, honest, faithful, socially responsible, life-serving, and joyous. Central to these values is the gospel's law of love.[2]

This does not mean that all sexual behaviors should be blindly accepted. The theologians who wrote this book suggest that a given sexual activity is not intrinsically immoral but must be judged by the criteria stated above; however, the ideal context for heterosexual expression is still to be the marital bond. But Nelson tells us this teaching.

> . . . has been criticized on the grounds that its major norm of "creative growth toward integration" and its seven value criteria for measuring sexual acts are too general: they could apply to

---

[1] Kosnick, Anthony, *et al. Human Sexuality: New Directions in American Catholic Thought*, Paramus, N.J.: Paulist/Newman Press, 1976.

[2] Nelson, James B. *Between Two Gardens: Reflections on Sexuality and Religious Experience*, New York: Pilgrim Press, 1983, pp. 60–61.

any human actions and are not specifically enough related to the distinctive arena of sexuality.[3]

Some critics have argued that the liberal interpretation of the statements of the Second Vatican Council would make it possible to interpret almost any sexual act as moral provided no one gets hurt. Defenders have argued that the context within which the sexual act occurs cannot realistically be ignored when trying to determine issues of morality. Maybe because we are not theologians but look at these issues from the perspective of less theologically trained persons, it seems to us that both sides are right! The problem seems to be this: How can moral guidelines be utilized in the absence of legalistic, inflexible and precise definitions? This problem is not new, it did not begin with the Second Vatican Council, and it is not limited to Roman Catholicism. It is certainly present in Protestantism. We have not intentionally ignored Protestant problems but share with Nelson this impression of the Protestant position on sex:

> Sexuality in Protestantism is a fascinating and confusing picture. While in Jewish and Roman Catholic traditions there are divergent views and emphases, within Protestantism this is multiplied manyfold. With an enormous denominational diversity, with the absence of a central ecclesiastical teaching authority, with differing convictions on biblical interpretation and on the weight to be given to contemporary sources, it is even more difficult to speak meaningfully of a "Protestant position" on sexuality than with the other major faith groups.[4]

In presenting his own views on what an emerging Protestant sexual ethic may look like, Nelson comes to the position that it is probably unrealistic to look for absolute rules that can cover all situations, since rules based on biblical times may not be

---

[3] *Ibid.*, p. 61.
[4] *Ibid.*, p. 65.

able to cover all modern conditions in which individuals have to make sexual choices. As we mentioned in Chapter 2, Nelson believes that "The antidote to legalism is an ethics that finds its center and direction in *love* rather than in a series of specific, absolute injunctions."[5] Love is a central concept in Nelson's formulations of a methodology for sexual decision making, just as the "gospel's law of love" is central, among some Catholic theologians, to the values that give meaning to specific sexual acts.

In private correspondence with us, Professor Nelson clarified some of the points he brought out in his book concerning the complex nature of the relationship between love and sexual acts:

> God made us sexual beings not simply to procreate the race, but even more fundamentally to draw us out of loneliness into communication and communion with others. "Eros" (our love which yearns for our own fulfillment) is important as well as "agape" (self-giving love). That means that healthy self-love (which is fundamentally different from selfishness or egocentricity) is basic to our capacity to give ourselves caringly to others. Love that expresses itself in responsible sexuality, then, is self-affirming, caring of others' well-being, honest, faithful to ongoing relationships, and life-giving.[6]

While we would agree with Professor Nelson, his comments raise a serious problem. We *think* we understand what he means by the words he uses—but we have the advantage that we have read his books as well as many others in this area. We cannot assume that others have done the same. Thus, sometimes true and important concepts and ideas may be misinterpreted or ignored due to a lack of understanding and knowledge—especially in so difficult an area as sex. It is encouraging to note the similarities in his thinking with that of many of the

---

[5] *Ibid.*, p. 81.
[6] Nelson, James B. Private correspondence. December 14, 1987.

contemporary Catholic and Jewish theologians. But the problem is this: If nothing else, the strict rules that governed sexual conduct in the past had the virtue of simplicity (although not always consistency and compassion). In contrast, the flexibility of Nelson's solution makes things more complex and harder to define. His formulations are centered around the concept of Christian love and utilize basic moral principles of the Bible, while at the same time they take into consideration the implications of the strict "legalistic" approach and its apparent *rejection* in the modern world.[7] We are sure that there are many religious leaders and parents who fear that the lack of strict rules, precisely defined, could result in a state of sexual "normlessness." Is there a way of resolving this issue? Perhaps.

This conflict between legalism and normlessness is a fundamental problem facing almost all religions and denominations today in many controversial areas of sexuality and sex-related behaviors. Joseph Fletcher, formerly Dean of St. Paul's Cathedral in Cincinnati and professor of social ethics at the Episcopal Theology School in Cambridge, Massachusetts, stated this problem clearly over two decades ago:

> There are at bottom only three alternative routes or approaches to follow in making moral decisions. They are: (1) the legalistic; (2) the antinomian, the opposite extreme—i.e., a lawless or unprincipled approach; and (3) the situational. All three have played their part in the history of Western morals, legalism being by far the most common and persistent. Just as legalism triumphed among the Jews after the exile, so, in spite of Jesus's and Paul's revolt against it, it has managed to dominate Christianity constantly from very early days.[8]

Fletcher describes "legalism" as morality based on "not just the spirit but the letter of the law. Its principles, codified in

---

[7] Nelson, 1983, p. 81.
[8] Fletcher, Joseph. *Situation Ethics: The New Morality*, Philadelphia: Westminster Press, 1966, p. 17.

rules, are not merely guidelines or maxims to illuminate the situation; they are *directives* to be followed. Solutions are preset . . ." and can often be looked up in a book to determine whether an act is moral or not.[9] Our communications with young people show that they perceive their religion's approach to sexuality to be "preset" in this way. Whether it is indeed so is not as relevant as the fact that this is how people perceive their religion. Furthermore, they feel it oppressive enough to make them have to decide for themselves what *they* consider to be moral. Of course, this would not apply to all young people who identify with a religion.

Antinomianism is posited by Fletcher as a kind of polar opposite of legalism:

> This is the approach with which one enters into the decision-making armed with no principles or maxims whatsoever, to say nothing of *rules*. In every "existential moment" or "unique" situation, it declares, one must rely on the situation itself, *there and then*, to provide its ethical solution.[10]

Although Fletcher writes about antinomianism in intellectual, philosophical and theological terms, it is our impression that young boys and girls (and their older brothers and sisters as well as parents) often make the wrong choices regarding sexual activities because of their antinomianistic approach; that is, they lack a moral code to bring to the situation. It appears to us that if one rejects the perceived oppressiveness of religious codes, one is left with very little moral reasoning other than an informal antinomianism.

Fletcher believes that the solution to prevent a growing antinomianism in our society is situation ethics—an approach where "[one] enters into every decision-making situation fully armed with the ethical maxims of his community and its

---

[9] *Ibid.*, p. 18.
[10] *Ibid.*, p. 22.

heritage, and he treats them with respect as illuminators of his problems," to be understood, however, in the context of the biblical command to love.[11]

A methodology inherent in situation ethics for moral decision making is developed throughout Fletcher's book. He bases this method on a set of six propositions:

1. Only one "thing" is intrinsically good; namely, love: nothing else at all.
2. The ruling norm of Christian decision is love: nothing else.
3. Love and justice are the same, for justice is love distributed, nothing else.
4. Love wills the neighbor's good whether we like him or not.
5. Only the end justifies the means; nothing else.
6. Love's decisions are made situationally, not prescriptively.[12]

Fletcher explains each proposition in a separate chapter and offers suggestions for how four factors (the end, the means, the motives and the consequences) can be used to analyze problematic situations. Together this provides the reader with a compelling argument for the possibility of resolving moral questions in a changing world. His approach appears to be especially useful as a means for teaching people how to exercise moral thinking when there is not always a simple right or wrong standard to use. For example, he uses this story, which he titles "sacrificial adultery" to urge readers to put on their moral thinking caps:

> As the Russian armies drove westward [in WWII] . . . a Soviet patrol picked up a Mrs. Bergmeier foraging food for her three children . . . and without any clear reason for it, she was taken to a prison camp in the Ukraine. Her husband had been captured [by the Allied Army] and was a prisoner in Wales.

---

[11] *Ibid.*, p. 26.
[12] *Ibid.*, pp. 57, 69, 87, 103, 120, 134.

When he returned to Berlin, he . . . round[ed] up his children
. . . [ages 15, 12, 10]. Their mother's whereabouts remained a
mystery, but they never stopped searching. She more than
anything else was needed to reknit them as a family in that dire
situation of hunger, chaos and fear.

Meanwhile, in the Ukraine, Mrs. Bergmeier learned . . . that
her husband and family were trying to keep together and find
her. But the rules allowed them to release her for only two
reasons: (1) illness needing medical facilities beyond the camp's,
in which case she would be sent to a Soviet hospital elsewhere,
and (2) pregnancy, in which case she would be returned to
Germany as a liability.

She . . . finally asked a friendly . . . guard to impregnate her,
which he did. Her condition being medically verified, she was
sent back to Berlin and her family. They welcomed her with
open arms, even when she told them how she had managed it.
When the child was born, they loved him . . . [and took] him to
be christened. . . . After the ceremony . . . [they] sat down in
the pastor's study, to ask him whether they were right to feel
[as morally right] as they did. . . . Should they be grateful to
the . . . [camp guard]? Had Mrs. Bergmeier done a good and
right thing?[13]

The more we think about this incident, the more important
it seems to be able to consider it with Fletcher's four factors—
end, means, motives and consequences—before jumping to a
moral conclusion. And, if more people engaged in these kinds
of considerations, would not there be a greater likelihood of
minimizing inappropriate and destructive *choices* for many in
the area of sexual behavior?

It seems to us that contemporary movements in Judaism,
Catholicism and much of Protestantism are headed in the
direction of some kind of situation or context ethic. One
problem that seems to impede progress in this area is that
some critics seem to view situation ethics and religion as

---

[13]*Ibid.*, pp. 164–165.

antithetical. They apparently reject the notion that situation ethics can be a methodology *within* Judaism and Christianity. They also seem to confuse situation ethics within a religious framework with antinomianism, which is independent of a religious underpinning.

Of course, there are some religions and religious groups that are not grappling with the problem of situation ethics and do not have much ambivalence about taking a firm position on what is right and what is wrong behavior in the area of sexuality—the orthodox in both Judaism and Catholicism, the Fundamentalist Protestant denominations, the Muslims, and others. In particular, we have been impressed by the manner in which the Church of Jesus Christ of Latter-Day Saints (the Mormons) has approached the difficult task of teaching moral and ethical precepts in the area of sexuality. If Jews, Italians, Chinese and Japanese, among other groups, may be said to be child-centered societies, the Mormons must be said to be family-centered, *par excellence*. There appears to be a structured, systematic, integrated and total approach to morality through the family. Thus, sexual morality is taught as part of a system and way of life that focuses on the goal of eternal or celestial marriage. The church reaches out to the family through many media: songs, family meetings, family resource books, television, videos, etc., to provide the Mormon perspective on all aspects of sexuality for all family members. In some ways, this emphasis on a *system* of morality, mainly taught within the family, from childhood on, is similar to what Hassidim and other Orthodox Jews do when they teach their children the law of *Talmud* and religious obligations within the family at the very earliest ages of three and four.

It is not our place to declare one sexual ethic and criterion for moral behavior better than another. Our point is that the way in which the moral code (whatever it may be) is implemented in decision making and translated into actual behavior must be clear enough for lay persons to understand, apply and transmit to their children. In the absence of strict legalistic

109

pronouncements, a methodology for moral decision making *must* be available to the average person if we expect him or her to make responsible choices.

In doing our research for this book, we were dismayed at the sight of theologians writing for theologians, while interpreters talk down to parents and young people about the "new" meaning of sexuality in this or that religion. We do not wish to offend the professional religious writers who try to reach the public, but are they shaping the public in their own image? Do they really think that the young girl of 13 who has just become pregnant would not have done so if she had read their articles? Do they think that her parents are any more capable of understanding what they are talking about than the young girl? Do they think that preaching abstinence until one has a loving, responsible, mature, etc., relationship has any functional meaning to most people in our society? It appears as if the moral code and system is for the elite to understand, but the masses must still obey because they must obey. And we wonder why youths seem so irresponsible! *They and their family have not been taught a systematic moral code in a manner that is understandable and applicable.*

If one grows up with no religious identity and continues to remain without a religious commitment, then the legitimate source of one's morality is somewhat different from that of a more religious counterpart. But one still needs a moral code, and the problem of who teaches the sexual standards is the same. Are these standards being taught in the religious community, at home, in school or where? Has the problem of moral decision making become so complex that young persons cannot grapple with it and arrive at wise choices in the area of sexuality? We don't think so. It may be that there is a professional or intellectual gap that accounts for the weakness in our moral training.

If we look at the growing body of literature in the social sciences, we find that much is known about the how's, why's and wherefore's of young children learning moral reasoning

110

and judgments. The work of the late Professor Lawrence Kohlberg of Harvard on moral development and thinking among children has received much attention in the academic and social science communities.[14] (See David Goslin's comprehensive book *Handbook of Socialization Theory and Research*[15] for a well-rounded collection of writings on how children, adolescents and adults become "civilized.") It isn't that we don't know how to develop moral reasoning, but that we hardly ever apply good educational principles in the appropriate settings of school, church and home. (More on this throughout the remaining chapters.)

And, finally, we believe that the clearest and yet most profound statement of the problem that we all must address as parents and educators and sexual beings, in the area of sexual morality, was told to us by the charismatic Paul Moore, Jr., the Episcopal Bishop of New York—a man with enormous social concern and compassion:

What I have said . . . is that you must take the overall message of the Bible—of compassion, justice, mercy, forgiveness, peace and dignity—and then you factor in the present social conditions of the world we live in and [determine] how they meet in the question of the particulars of morality. Therefore, since in our society kids are maturing much earlier than we did and because of economic conditions [they] cannot be married sometimes until they are [in their late twenties]. . . . What do they do with fifteen years of sexual drive which is the strongest of anytime in their life? What do we do about that? What is the best thing for those kids and for society? . . . I think that if you can have kids understand that their sexual morality should be on the same basis as their other morality—namely: Are you hurting the other person? Are you exploiting the other person? Are

---

[14] In particular, see Kohlberg, Lawrence. *Stages in the Development of Moral Thought and Action*, New York: Holt, Rinehart, and Winston, 1969.
[15] Goslin, David A., editor. *Handbook of Socialization Theory and Research*, Chicago: Rand McNally, 1969.

you being honest with the other person? . . . Are [you] breaking the commandment to love your God and to love your neighbor: is your action a loving thing for you, for your neighbor and for God? These are the kinds of questions all morality is based on.

We hope this brief interlude has helped summarize and clarify some of the recurrent themes of this book—those that we feel are the most pervasive and the most important. When you finish reading the rest of the chapters, come back to this theoretical interlude and read it again; we think you will have a new perspective on these somewhat complicated issues.

CHAPTER 7

Adultery:
From Cheating to Swinging

When President Jimmy Carter was interviewed by *Playboy* magazine in November, 1976, he startled many people with his honest admission that even though he was a married adult, there were occasions when he had had "lust" in his heart—but he had not let these feelings carry over to his behavior. This comment must have struck home to many men and women who might have thought that there was something terribly wrong about even a loving faithful spouse sometimes "lusting" or at least thinking about wanting to have sex with someone other than his or her spouse. But this should not surprise anyone because a little common sense would tell us that a marriage vow cannot turn off sexual desires; if it did, it would also turn off desires for the spouse. Obviously, the notion that a vow can selectively turn off hormonal and nervous system response so as to limit attraction only to the spouse and no one else does not seem plausible. Having thoughts should not frighten us into thinking that we must or will act upon them. Although most of us are able to control these thoughts and feelings, some of us cannot. As evidenced by the recent behavior of several public figures, there are those who cannot, or choose not to, control their lust and do allow their fantasies to carry

113

over to their actions. Thus, from biblical times to the present, adultery has been a real fear and concern for millions of people. It's even proscribed by a biblical commandment.

Of all the areas of sexual morality we discuss in this book, the only one specifically forbidden by one of the Ten Commandments is adultery: *THOU SHALL NOT COMMIT ADULTERY.* Another Commandment, *THOU SHALL NOT COVET THY NEIGHBOR'S WIFE*, indirectly bans similar behavior.

In biblical Jewish law (based on Leviticus 20:10), adultery applied only to the sexual intercourse of either a married woman with a man other than her husband or a man with someone else's wife. It did not apply to a married man who had sex with an unmarried woman. Thus, according to the law, a woman could be granted a divorce if she caught her husband having sex with another *married* woman (providing there were sufficient witnesses) but not with an unmarried woman.[1] A similar double standard existed in both ancient Greece and Rome until the period of early Christianity, when for the first time adultery was penalized equally for men and for women. But according to psychologist Bernard Murstein, the purpose of this was not to right a wrong for women but rather to discourage sexual activity for both men and women.[2] Though in principle the laws equally punished men and women, in practice the church officials often urged the wife to forgive her adulterous husband but heaped much condemnation on the adulterous wife, who was often rejected and thrown out of the household by her husband.[3]

After centuries of alternating leniency and repressiveness, by the seventeenth century moral standards had again become somewhat lenient, and as the English legal commander William Blackstone noted: "the temporal courts, therefore, take no

---

[1] Murstein, Bernard I. *Love, Sex and Marriage Through the Ages,* New York: Springer, 1974, p. 43.
[2] *Ibid.,* p. 95.
[3] *Ibid.,* p. 99.

cognizance of the crime of adultery, otherwise than as a private injury."[4] The historian Vern Bullough commented on these changes:

> In surveying the history of royalty from the last part of the seventeenth until almost the end of the eighteenth century, it seems as if kings had to have mistresses as part of the mark of their royalty. Henry IV . . . was alleged to have had some fifty-six mistresses. The most famous [mistress of Louis XIV] was . . . Madame de Pompadour.[5]

Among the European nobility of the time, there was no secret that many ladies kept two "husbands," one in name and one for sex, while mate swapping began to become popular in France.[6]

In the American colonies, the influence of the Puritans was making itself felt. The Puritans didn't belong to any one particular religion, but they appear to have been a combination of people from some of the Protestant denominations, especially Presbyterians, Congregationalists, Quakers and some others who were dissatisfied with certain aspects of traditional religious groups. Above all, they seem to have been concerned with sexual morality. In this context, adultery was particularly repugnant, and some Puritan colonies passed statutes making it punishable by death, as was rape, sodomy and bestiality.[7] Gradually, these rarely invoked severe penalties were replaced by public humiliation: flogging, branding and the infamous "scarlet letter *A*," and later by a fine or short imprisonment. In spite of these stated prohibitions, famous Americans, including Benjamin Franklin, Thomas Jefferson and Alexander

---

[4] Blackstone, William. *Commentaries on the Law of England*, Philadelphia: Robert Bell, 1771, IV, p. 65. Quoted in Vern L. Bullough, *Sexual Variance in Society and History*, Chicago: The University of Chicago Press, 1976, p. 466.

[5] Bullough, pp. 466, 467.

[6] Murstein, p. 230.

[7] Bullough, pp. 504–507.

Hamilton (our equivalent of the European nobility) had known adulterous liaisons without much damage to their reputations.[8]

As we moved through the nineteenth and twentieth centuries, punishment for adultery seemed less and less a social concern, and by the middle of the twentieth century it was lessened merely to grounds for obtaining a divorce. But this reduction of punishment apparently did not result from a similar reduction of the frequency of adultery in our society. (While one may argue that the reduction in punishment may have caused an increase in adultery, there is nothing in the literature to substantiate any cause and effect relationship.) On the contrary, the high rate of adultery was made apparent when the Kinsey data became available:

On the basis of these active data, and allowing for the cover-up that has been involved, it is probably safe to suggest that about half of all the married males have intercourse with women other than their wives, at some time while they are married.[9]

The accumulative incidences [for married women] . . . reached their maximum of 26 percent by forty years of age.[10]

So it seems we have always had adultery, and observers of the sexual scene today might say that if we were to repeat the study Kinsey did forty years ago, we would probably find the rates now to be much higher. But in the late 1960s, during the so-called sexual revolution, a new twist appeared: swinging. This trend encouraged "open marriages" and mate swapping as acceptable diversions and even good for some marriages, rather than as dangerous violations of a necessary and tradi-

---

[8] Murstein, pp. 318–319.
[9] Kinsey, Alfred C., W. Pomeroy, and C. Martin. *Sexual Behavior in the Human Male*, Philadelphia: W. B. Saunders, 1948, p. 585.
[10] Kinsey, Alfred C., W. Pomeroy, C. Martin, and P. Gebhard, *Sexual Behavior in the Human Female*, Philadelphia: W. B. Saunders, 1953, p. 416.

tional moral standard. For many persons, what had formerly been secretive and marriage threatening—cheating on one's spouse—was now permissible and even justifiable. How and why did this come about?

When we look back at the late 1960s and the early 1970s with that great analytic tool hindsight, it appears that the much touted "sexual revolution" hardly deserves such an extreme title. A few more percentage points of unmarried young men and women engaged in sex; some couples openly advocated what many had formerly done in privacy (mate swapping); women acknowledged in open discussion what they had previously sought with a sense of discomfort (full orgasmic response). All this hardly qualifies as a "revolution," but as an evolutionary trend—yes!

It seems to us that the apparent "radical" sexual changes and upheavals of the sexual revolution that took place in some areas of sexuality did not take place in the area of sexual *behavior*; rather, we would suggest that a true attempt at a revolution took place, with partial success, in sexual *semantics*. Many sexual activities, which people in unknown numbers have probably engaged in since civilization first developed, were being viewed by participants and spokespersons as legitimate and acceptable rather than dirty, evil, immoral, sinful and perverted. Indeed, if there is any sense to be made out of this period, it is that it reflected a basic wish of people to be seen as moral for the physical expression of their love and biological urges. That is, what appeared to be a monolithic moral code, which condemned any sexual expression outside of the traditional heterosexual monogamous marital relationship, was being challenged. We don't believe that the behavior had necessarily changed but that many people were tired of feeling guilty because their sexual behaviors and feelings did not fit the desired stereotype.

We believe that the same conditions that helped prompt this "erotic revolutions" as the poet and novelist Lawrence Lipton

117

described it at that time,[11] still prevail and also that people today have the same need for moral approval that they have always had. This is not to suggest that we create a "new morality" to fit the needs of today's generation, but, on the contrary, whatever the sexual choices are, they should be made out of consideration of moral values in addition to the more common emotional impulses. But once again, one cannot consider these moral values and act upon them if one is not first taught them in an understandable fashion. It seems that we cannot help but repeat: Most young people appear never to have learned sexual morality, only sexual repressiveness and prohibition.

To understand why traditional formulations of sexual morality seem to have weakened as major guidelines in helping people, particularly young people, make appropriate choices, we have to look at the fundamental changes in the family that have taken place as we moved from an agrarian to an industrial society. We will see how the shift away from an inward family focus and self-sufficiency to a more external and social institutional *weltanschauung* (world view) has weakened family ties and made the temptations and availability of adultery more real. These temptations and availability have, in turn, weakened the family still further, leading not only to more divorces but also to an overall deterioration of a moral support system from within the family. How did this happen?

If we look at the portrayal of the family in biblical days and for much of the history of Western culture, we see that the original functions of the family, that is, the main things that families did for people, are far from what the functions are today. What are these functions, how were they related to the transmission of moral sexual standards and in what ways have they changed? In order to make it easier to understand, think

---

[11] For an interesting analysis of the moral issues in question at that time, see Lipton, Lawrence. *The Erotic Revolution: An Affirmative View of the New Morality*, Los Angeles: Sherbourne Press, Inc., 1965.

118

of one of the groups who live in different parts of the United States and who have kept a very traditional family and religious lifestyle, such as the Amish, the Hutterites or the Hassidic Jews.

Sociologists and anthropologists have said that we can view the traditional family functions as fitting into at least seven broad categories: sexual gratification, reproduction, economic, education, recreation, religious, and social-psychologic. In essence, this means that all vital sustaining forces came from within the traditional family. Sexual gratification was restricted to the husband-wife relationship. Recreational and religious activities were practiced within the family or among close families from the same background. Even education and economic sustenance (securing food, clothing, and shelter) remained largely in the domain of the family or extended family. It is easy to understand how the traditional family was able to pass on values and sexual morality from generation to generation and have enough community supervision so that most people probably followed the expected sexual behavior. It certainly seems that in a traditional family structure, with the family taking on so many of the responsibilities and functions we see delegated to outside authorities and institutions today, family members looked inward and toward the extended family of grandparents, uncles, aunts and cousins as role models as well as for the resolution of social behavior and value uncertainties.

Today we see quite a different picture of the family, particularly in the urban areas of our country. For good or bad, depending on your perspective, the changes that have taken place for most families living in modern Western society have indeed been extensive: In the modern economy, the father tends to work outside of the home or farm and often spends considerable time with people who are different in many ways— religiously, politically and socially, and, perhaps with different values, ethics and behaviors in the area of sexuality. Frequently, these people with whom the father/husband interacts in the workplace are women who themselves may be mothers/wives.

119

Now both the husband and the wife are in professional situations in which they must interact professionally with both men and women. Friendships can become romantic through a mutuality of work interests and by associating with a colleague on a daily basis, sometimes spending more time together than with the spouse. Whether it is 50 or 60 or 70 percent of all married women who are out of the home and working is not the issue. Suffice it to say that it has become the norm for married women to work, irrespective of the reason or current statistics. Back in the early 1970s Lou Lieberman conducted a study in a large Southern city where he found that married women who were currently working and single women who were studying at college in anticipation of a career while married were much more likely to consider the likelihood of having an extramarital affair than married or single women who wanted to be economically dependent on their husbands. He believed that this reflected less fear on the part of working women for the economic consequences of divorce.[12]

Concern for childcare has moved from the mother, not over to the extended family of relatives because they too are working or no longer living in the same community, but to day care and nursery schools. Increases in leisure time due to shorter work days and longer vacations seem to result in people wanting to do and see "new" things: to travel, to meet and experience new friends, to engage in recreation that their parents never dreamed of—going to a ski lodge, renting videos that may reflect lifestyles and values foreign to their own, watching how the "other half lives" on TV, taking courses in adult education programs in which they meet different people, getting in the car and driving somewhere for the weekend and meeting new people at a dance or bar, etc. Religious value training is assumed to be left to the churches: youth groups, Sunday school and released-time programs in which children leave their public

---

[12] Lieberman, Louis. "Economic Security and Extramarital Sex," presented at the Southern Sociological Association meetings, Athens, Georgia, 1973.

school to attend a local religious education program (sometimes for as little as one hour a week). Rarely does the "modern" family seem to have time for religion except at church for one hour a week (compared to twenty or thirty hours a week they may spend watching TV).

In short, while the traditional family looked inward or toward the extended family for social and recreational activities, the modern family looks outward. Today, the family is assumed to be primarily for having children and the sexual/emotional relationship of the wife and husband for each other. In a society in which marriage partners are accustomed to looking outward rather than inward, any strain that might develop in the relationship between the husband and wife (a normal occurrence at any time in history, we are sure) may be very difficult to resolve. Rather than working with each other to resolve the conflict, they may each believe that there is always someone else "out there" who can make a better partner.

As we indicated earlier in this chapter, it seems to us that the more significant change during the sexual revolution of two decades ago was semantic rather than behavioral. There was some increase in nontraditional sexual behavior, but, more importantly, many people wanted acceptance of what they had already been doing—behavior that had been frowned upon or condemned. An extreme example of this attempt at legitimizing deviant behavior was the many "swingers clubs"—organizations where married couples could meet each other and exchange spouses for an evening of sex, in private or in a group. In these groups, there was mutual reinforcement that their values were "better" than traditional values because they were more "honest." They reinforced the notion to one another (and occasionally to the public via mass media) that they were "preserving the family" by engaging in this rather than getting divorced. The body of literature concerning swinging clearly shows the attempts to turn what has historically been considered adultery and thus immoral, into a "new morality."

The irony in their perspective is that many couples in our

121

society who do have sex problems often degenerate into loveless marriages or feel the pressures to get divorced. What has happened is not that swinging has become legitimized and moral but divorce has. It appears that adultery is still unacceptable to most people, but divorce is almost at the stage of being considered an expected outcome of urban marriages. Thus, it appears to us, a person feeling trapped in a troubled marriage may now more easily choose divorce or adultery. Both choices are bad, but the realization that one can always get divorced may make the choice of adultery even more appealing when problems, particularly sex problems, appear in the marriage—this, of course, only increases the likelihood that the marriage will get worse. Contrary to what common sense may tell some people, we do not believe that divorce is often the *result* of adultery (there are numerous reasons for divorce unrelated to adultery), but rather that because divorce has become so easy an option in our society, combined with the outward orientation of so many couples, adultery is no longer as feared as we might have thought. Thus, the moral aspects must become all the more important. This tragic state of affairs in which marital discord easily awakens thoughts of divorce cannot be taken lightly. The argument that it is better to raise children in a loving one-parent family than in a hateful two-parent family may be true in any given case. But if we take a broader perspective and look at the importance of the intact family, we should, as a nation, be doing something about the problem of the weakening family. The issues involved are at the center of what this book is all about: How do we learn to make the right *choices* in life, particularly in emotional and stressful situations? We don't have the answers, but we will keep trying to raise everyone's consciousness that we must begin the process of finding answers.

Despite the fact that the Commandment not to commit adultery is probably known by almost every adult from a Judeo-Christian or other religious background, in general, the persons we talked with said very little about their religious attitudes concerning adultery. Instead, rather vague disapproval was given. For example, a young woman tells us:

> All I ever heard in my family [about adultery] were comments made by my parents about the concept of "open marriage" which was somewhat in fashion in the 1960s and 1970s and that was that they didn't approve and it was not to be done.

For some, it wasn't so much what the parents said but their personal observations of the parental and familial relationship that was the moral message:

> When my parents were living together, before they got divorced, they never saw anyone else. There was no one that broke up their marriage—I know this for a fact. They never cheated. I know that. I feel so strongly about that. Extramarital sex is just wrong. It should not be done. I've seen so many marriages go down the tubes. I don't want to get married until I know I can be so completely in love with somebody that I will have no desire to sleep with anybody else. I don't look at it from a religious perspective, but I think that I get this strong moral feeling about extramarital affairs from my sense of family. Family is so important to me that I wouldn't do anything to threaten it.

It is important to note that even though the parents' marriage broke up, the positive image of family and fidelity stayed with this woman. A young man gave us this very insightful explanation of why he wouldn't want to cheat on his wife, which involved different dimensions of ethics and values:

> There are two reasons why I wouldn't have extramarital sex— one, I love my wife very much, and two, I don't want to get AIDS.

We pointed out to him that neither of these reasons appears to have derived from moral bases (one being based on affection

123

SEX AND MORALITY

and fear of loss and the other on fear of disease) and asked
whether there might be a deeper moral basis for his contemporary views on adultery:

> In terms of morals, I feel—and this is where a little bit of my
> old Catholic morality comes in—that unless there is something
> wrong with your marriage and you realize there is a problem,
> you picked this person to be your wife, bedmate and best friend.
> I'm one of these persons who doesn't feel right when I'm
> cheating in any area: on an exam, at work, or any area. It's not
> so much a religious issue, because . . . I saw priests and nuns
> cheating on their vows, and I was not impressed by religious
> morality. Basically, it is because I want to be able to get up and
> look myself in the mirror every morning. Now because of the
> nature of the work that I do [with many opportunities for
> corruption], I feel I have to keep a certain moral standpoint for
> myself because it is easy on my job to become corrupt.

We asked him where these nonmarital moral standards came
from:

> I think that a lot of them come from my father during my
> formative years, because my father was, during all his years on
> the police department, an honest cop. When he died as a
> lieutenant, we didn't have a lot of money. We lived in a rent-
> controlled apartment, no big bank accounts, no house on Long
> Island, no car. He was a man who firmly believed in the old
> things like "Honesty is the best policy," "Thou shall not lie."
> This was all taught to me by example and punishment, but he
> was a firm believer in Catholicism and a strong churchgoer. I'm
> sure that a lot of his moral beliefs reflected this.

Of course, we applaud this young man's values, consistent
with his ethical and moral beliefs, but it is sad to note that this
was one of the few times that anyone gave even partial credit
to their religion for lasting moral guideposts—and even here
the praise was mixed with much disapproval of what he saw

124

as religious models. It is important to learn from his answers that morality in one area of human conduct is not an isolated experience. In a sense, morality of one type for one area reinforces or helps provide models for exercise of morality in other areas. This is why we believe in the significance of developing the moral decision-making skills for very young people because we are sure that lack of them inhibits later moral behaviors in the nonsexual adult world.

A young woman also tells us of how parental modelling was the dominant moral message for her:

> My father never talked to me about sex except for once when we were talking about marriage and he said that cheating was the worst thing possible for a marriage. He said: "In all honesty, I've never had an affair. I love your mother too much. I would never do that to her." He believes that marriage is a sacred thing and even if a man didn't love his wife, he still shouldn't have an affair. I think this had something to do with a friend of his who was having an affair and just got divorced.

Although they do not consider adulterous affairs examples of moral behavior, some people may accept them as one of the harsh realities of married life. In this way, cultural attitudes may have a stronger influence on the tolerance for traditionally immoral behaviors such as adultery. The assumption that only men "cheat" in their community and "that's life" is reflected by these two young women from Puerto Rico:

> Whenever we heard about anyone having an affair, or that a marriage broke up, it was always that "he" found another woman, never "she." I remember, as I was growing up, a few of my friends had parents who got divorced. I'm not sure if it really was because of another woman, but it was assumed by my parents that it was because of another woman . . . [but still,] my mother would say that: "It was wrong, because if you are married, you are married to just one other person." I think that you also learn it's wrong by just going to weddings as a child

125

and know what marriage meant: that you give yourselves to each other and exclusively to each other.

An apparent tolerance of male infidelity is told by the second woman:

I was never taught about adultery from a religious point of view, but when I was growing up, I knew of a number of people where the husband was cheating on the wife. Usually, there was a lot of pity felt for the woman and the guy, well, "that's what guys do to their women. It's a very macho thing to do and even though it's not very nice to do it—he's a man." I never discussed this with my family or friends, but I would hear it as gossip. In one case, in this small town where I lived, a man I knew had at least five other women in town, that his wife knew about, with kids and all. But he was able to support them all. Did people consider it immoral? Definitely not! No one ever talked about it as being immoral, at least not any of the people I knew of. Some people just thought of it as being disgusting, but it just wasn't looked at as being moral or immoral. He was able to support them all because he was one of the richest men in town. Many people, though, just look the other way when a man cheats on his wife. I even remember my mother once telling me something along the lines of: "Carmela, you know sometimes men want to have other women. That happens, don't worry about it." This was in reference to the boyfriend I was going out with at the time. She was sort of telling me I had to be tolerant of that—even if he goes with another woman.

The issue of adultery and the teaching of moral principles related to it are both simple and complex at the same time. It is simple from the religious perspective (or from a legal, secular contract if sexual exclusiveness is part of the contract) in that it is always a violation of marital vows or sacraments or contractual agreements. It is complex because changes have taken place in our industrial and urbanized world that psychologically tempt or pull marital partners away from each other. A list of some of the factors placing strain on marital fidelity:

- Little fear from unwanted pregnancy due to effective contraceptives,
- A longer span of vigorous, healthy life,
- Increasing numbers of wives entering the labor force,
- Greater amount of leisure time for husbands and wives,
- Cultural obsession with youthful activities,
- Decline of religious control and influence,
- Psychological tensions due to international crises and threats, creating for some a hedonistic "eat, drink and be merry for tomorrow we may be dead" attitude,
- Decline in social controls with concomitant rise of peer influence,
- Urbanization and decrease in general community scrutiny,
- Increase in persons getting higher education, particularly women, thus increasing their exposure to alternative and nontraditional lifestyles,
- A general questioning of traditional religious sexual values, even by the religious,
- Increasing affluence for all classes, thus more money to spend for "fun,"
- Increased media-generated sexual stimulation,
- Continuing emphases upon individual satisfaction and fulfillment.

While we applaud some of the above and decry others, it is not hard to understand that we must live with all of these changes and influences and that we are not likely to go back to a simpler time in our history. We do not suggest that these factors should in any way legitimize adultery or modify traditional moral precepts. We offer them in order to underscore the need for methodologies, training and practice in moral decision making providing all of us with the skills to make wise moral choices.

CHAPTER 8

Birth Control: A Conflict of Moral Positions

Many people associate the name *Dr. Ruth* with *contraception*. Unfortunately, some of these people, mainly those who have not listened to the *Dr. Ruth* radio and TV shows, think that contraception is being stressed and encouraged so that young people can go ahead and have sex without the fear of consequences—as if sex itself was being encouraged. This is not at all the case. Dr. Westheimer advocates neither sex nor abstinence, but rather reasonable and considered *choices* in light of one's moral and religious beliefs as well as one's current life situation. Contraception is an issue for the married as well as the nonmarried. It is not a cold and technical mechanical imposition to prevent the miracle of conception but a moral decision regarding the life of both those who exist and those who may come to being. This is why we believe that birth control merits a separate chapter in our book on sex and morality and why we avoided a discussion of it in our earlier chapter on nonmarital sex.

   Historically, the values and ethics concerning the prevention of conception by artificial means were intertwined with more general attitudes and beliefs regarding sex, paternity, religion and medicine. At different times in history and in different

129

places, little distinction was made between birth control and abortion since the issue was really whether or not to allow a child to be born. Today, many people and religions in Western culture hold quite different moral sentiments and values about birth control and abortion. For this reason, we will treat abortion separately in the next chapter.

In the oldest of the known medical literatures, little distinction was made between pre- and postconceptive methods of birth control because the objective of both was to stop normal development following intercourse and before a pregnancy was obvious. As far back as the ancient Chinese medical texts of 5,000 years ago, there was discussion of preparations used to prevent a pregnancy from developing—and these preparations were not new even at that time. Ancient literature contains many references to recipes for making substances to induce menstruation in case a suspected pregnancy occurred.[1]

The ancient Egyptians used a variety of substances to prevent conception—some we now believe to be somewhat effective while others may have even promoted the fertilization. For example, some people inserted crocodile dung, honey or a resinous sap from the acacia plant into the vagina. Honey may have been mildly effective in lessening the motility of the sperm and acacia gum produces a lactic acid that may have worked as a spermicide, but crocodile dung, being slightly alkaline, might have neutralized vaginal acidity and even promoted the likelihood of conception! But regardless of the efficacy of a substance, or even of the danger, it seems that most cultures have always had some means available to try to prevent conception. Some were religiously and morally approved while others were not.

When we discussed Onanism in Chapter 3, we said in a footnote that most scholars now believe that the sin of Onan (refusing to carry out the custom of impregnating his dead

---

[1] Davis, Geoffrey. *Interception of Pregnancy*, London: Angus and Robertson, 1974, p. 119.

brother's wife) had to do with the act of *coitus interruptus* (withdrawal before ejaculation) rather than masturbation. This would imply that *coitus interruptus* became forbidden to the Jewish male as a method of birth control and that the religious taboo against birth control was male centered and not female centered. This is borne out by the fact that women were allowed to use some forms of contraception. In particular, women were permitted to insert a spongy substance called *mokh* into the vagina to prevent fertilization from taking place. The fact that women but not men were allowed to practice contraception may reflect the belief among the ancient Hebrews that the man was the source of the child and the womb was only the place where growth took place. But this does not explain *why* a man was not entitled to prevent pregnancy but a woman was.[2]

The issue of birth control was an important religious consideration from the earliest days of Christianity. Tertullian, one of the early Christian thinkers around the beginning of the third century A.D., had great influence over later Christian thinkers. His ideas are still reflected in the traditional Roman Catholic view of birth control that the use of chemicals and devices as a means of contraception is unnatural and hence carries some air of evil.[3]

Christian views on birth control were further shaped by St. Augustine who believed that the act of sex could be considered good only when it led to procreation; otherwise, it was evil. Therefore, since birth control was intended to stop the possibility of procreation and permit people to have sex just for pleasure, he considered it contrary to nature and therefore forbidden.[4]

The moral basis for considering birth control evil varied in different parts of the early Christian church. It appears that the Eastern branch of the church began to develop somewhat

---

[2] Bullough, Vern. *Sexual Variance in Society and History*, New York: Wiley, 1976, p. 79.
[3] Davis, p. 122.
[4] Bullough, pp. 194, 355.

different views on sexual intercourse. In the fourth century, St. John Chrysostom of the Eastern branch of Christianity wrote that he agreed with St. Augustine that marriage is the only way to prevent fornication but he did not believe that intercourse was necessarily a sin if it was not intended for the act of procreation. He reasoned that since the church did not forbid couples to engage in sex during old age or during the pregnancy of the wife, sex between husband and wife for pleasure alone, without intent to procreate, was not sinful. This did not give license to using contraceptives, however, because he also believed that it was God's will, along with the act of intercourse, that produced the conception. Therefore, using contraceptives would be an attempt to interfere with God's will and would be as serious a sin as homicide.[5] Even though this did not legitimize contraceptives, it probably did help somewhat at reducing sexual guilt feelings for those couples in the Eastern church who got a great deal of pleasure from sex.

Even then, as now, people found the ban on contraceptives not wholly acceptable. Some Eastern Christians must have practiced birth control following the medical recommendations of that time. For instance, Aetio, a Byzantine court physician of the sixth century, talked about preventing conception by having sex only during the days in the menstrual cycle considered to be "safer." He also mentioned other methods (but certainly not very effective ones) such as putting certain ointments on the cervix in order to close the cervical opening and prevent the sperm from entering the uterus. He even suggested the very dubious method of having men wash their penises with vinegar or a salt solution and for women to douche with the same liquids.[6] (We certainly hope no reader will think that these are effective to *any* degree, but unfortunately we still come across young people who have never been taught anything

---

[5] *Ibid.*, p. 324.
[6] *Ibid.*

132

about reliable contraceptives and who risk pregnancy thinking they are safe after a douche.)

In sixteenth century Europe, fears of widespread veneral disease led many to ignore the moral bans on using contraceptives in favor of a primitive form of a condom, a linen sheath. This was mainly to prevent disease, not conception, but undoubtedly some persons got the idea that it could also prevent a pregnancy. The first mention of a condom, using that word, made from animal membrane rather than linen was in the early 1700s. Again, this was discussed primarily in terms of its ability to help prevent syphilis rather than conception. Widespread interest in the use of these and other lesser known contraceptives received a boost at the beginning of the nineteenth century when interest in population control became more intense. Some people think that this was due to the influence of Thomas Malthus and his now famous Malthusian Theory in which he argued that the supply of food could only increase arithmetically but population could increase geometrically, leading to a situation in which the human population could soon outgrow the food supply. Although Malthus advocated limiting population through late marriage and abstinence from sex, others thought this unrealistic and advocated contraception as the best method to prevent the population explosion.[7]

In Chapter 5, we described the American "big shift" from a religious to a secular basis for sexual morality. We believe this shift paralleled the change in emphasis from on the prevention of disease to the prevention of conception that followed the distribution of the first vulcanized rubber condom. As we noted, changes in privacy and dating practices increased the possibility of pregnancy for unmarried women. As the advent of the condom and other methods of birth control, as well as effective antibiotics and other medications, alleviated

---

[7] *Ibid.*, pp. 549, 550.

fears of pregnancy and disease, sexual control among unmarried women had to be based on moral rather than physical considerations. The introduction of the first oral contraceptive in 1960 virtually eliminated any physical concerns about sexual activity. What remains are only moral concerns, but (as we have seen) these concerns are not always well defined or understood.

Since the 1960s little has occurred on the social or physical planes to back the traditional moral positions that one should not engage in sex outside of marriage and that one should not use contraception to prevent birth, whether married or not. Two exceptions come to mind: first, the obvious case of the 1. impact of AIDS that may prove increasingly more tragic before it can be controlled, and second, the lingering suspicion surrounding large-scale population control that resulted from the eugenics movement at the beginning of the twentieth century.

In the case of AIDS, while traditionalists may still argue that abstinence is the surest way of avoiding AIDS (and there is no quarreling with this position), it is unthinkable from a religious point of view to suggest that those who appear to be unable to abstain, out of choice or inability to make a choice, should suffer the punishment of AIDS rather than learn about the use of condoms to help prevent the disease. Surely, no one could suggest that the correct *moral* perspective is: If one cannot be abstinent, then the possibility of AIDS is preferable to a condom! We know that some may say that we are theologically naive in stating the issue in this manner. To this, we plead guilty, but nonetheless, the reality of the AIDS tragedy has forced many people to rethink various issues of morality and ethics. We will have more to say about this in Chapter 11.

2. The eugenics movement originally held the elitist and racist view that the upper classes should produce more children than the lower classes in order to improve the quality of human offspring. Even though the eugenics movement no longer exists to any degree today, some people from minority groups and

the Third World have argued that political activists who believe the economically poor should have fewer children to help them out of their poverty may be racially inspired. This is a real dilemma for our society because it turns out that those who are most likely to have children out of wedlock are those who are least able to afford and take care of them, placing even more burden on the mothers and making them less likely to get out of poverty.

It is unfortunate that sometimes the real issues get confused and people take political positions far removed from reality. In this case the reality is that birth control is a factor in what has become an increasing social problem: poverty among people of all colors in this country. On the cover of Senator Daniel Patrick Moynihan's new book, *Family and Nation*, there is the quotation: "For the first time in our history, children are the poorest age group in the population."[8] In this excellent and thoughtful book, Senator Moynihan reminds us that this is not to be viewed as solely a problem of minority groups:

> In round numbers, in 1984 half the poor in America (47.8 percent) lived in female-headed families. If the trend line of the past two decades has continued, as there is every reason to suppose, the 50 percent mark will by now have been reached. . . .
> Over half the 13.3 million poor children in America (62.9 percent) are white. Another third (33.1 percent) are black. One-sixth (17.7 percent) are of Spanish origin.[9]

Senator Moynihan is also very sensitive to the special burden that poverty places on the black community because of changes that have taken place in patterns of birth related to poverty:

---

[8] Moynihan, Daniel Patrick. *Family and Nation*, San Diego: Harcourt Brace Jovanovich, 1987.

[9] *Ibid.*, p. 96. Data from U.S. Bureau of the Census. *Money Income and Poverty Status of Families and Persons in the United States, 1984*, Washington, D.C.: U.S. Government Printing Office, 1985, pp. 3, 21, 22.

135

In 1985 Dorothy I. Height, president of the National Council of Negro Women, published an article in *Ebony*, "What Must Be Done about Children Having Children." She reports that while early marriage was common in the Black community in previous times, and hence early motherhood, "the statistical facts have changed dramatically in one area: Today an overwhelming majority of all Black children are born to single teenage mothers." If this is so, it obviously calls for a "mobilization"—Ms. Height's term—to deal with this "crisis." She cites Eleanor Holmes Norton: "It must be regarded as a natural catastrophe in our midst, a threat to the future of Black people without equal."[10]

Senator Moynihan goes on to cite data from the Guttmacher Institute (an independent nonprofit corporation for research, policy analysis and public education in the field of family planning) to point out that the crux of the problem today seems to be related to the increasing number of teenagers who get pregnant:

It is abundantly clear that teenagers in the United States are much more likely to become pregnant than are teenagers in other Western nations. The Alan Guttmacher Institute (1985) reports that the rate of teenage pregnancy among young American women aged 15–19 is 96 per 1,000. In Canada, the rate is 44 per 1,000 young women; the comparable rate in the Netherlands is 14 per 1,000. *Moreover, ours is the only developed nation in the world where rates of teenage pregnancy have been increasing of late* [emphasis ours].[11]

Is this a moral concern? Unquestionably! Is contraception the only answer? Of course not! If one is able to make the choice of abstinence until marriage, a perfectly viable option for many, then there is no need for *them* to be concerned with

---

[10] Moynihan, p. 167.
[11] *Ibid.*

contraception. But the reality that we must consider, as we have throughout this book, is that for many people, perhaps more so for the young, abstinence is not an option since *they were never provided with the moral framework* that must be drawn upon to *choose* abstinence. As we have seen, some parents believe that instilling fear is sufficient as a moral underpinning, but that only leads to social controls being absent when one doesn't believe that the parent will find out. Of course, there are some youngsters with strong moral and religious values who remain virgins out of choice and belief. Bravo to them. They are not the ones who are having children while still children themselves. Should we tell those who did not receive this important moral upbringing and who will not make the choice to remain abstinent: "We still don't want you to know about contraception—we would rather you have that child out of wedlock, even though you are only 14"? Is this a statement of morality? Perhaps. But whether it is or is not, let us have the moral education systematically taught to all youngsters to make them *morally literate,* since this form of illiteracy may be as destructive, if not more so, than *cultural illiteracy*.

It is necessary to teach a system of morality so that young people know what the morality is supposed to be *before* they engage in sex, not after the pregnancy has occurred. And, even for those whose religious commitment or lack of one does not regard either birth control or nonmarital sex as necessarily *immoral,* there are still times when it may be wrong to have sex—but this too must be based on an understandable moral message. For example, we regularly hear about a young woman, or man, who justifies having sex with a married person by claiming that this person's spouse is just not that interested in sex. Often therapists and counselors and sex educators will decry this because of the likelihood of the young woman or man being hurt by a no-win situation, but we believe that psychological explanations can be buttressed by moral reasoning. This can only occur when people are used to accepting the validity of moral reasoning, even in the absence of strong religious convictions. If the Bible did not say "Thou shall not commit adultery," would adultery be O.K.? Of course not, but ask your friends if they can exercise their moral faculties and come up with the *reason* why it would still be immoral? Some will be able to, but many will become confused when they are asked for the moral basis of sexuality without reference to traditional religion. This is because they were never taught a solid system of morality in which to function.

Confusion, or perhaps lack of moral reasoning, sometimes is transmitted with the best of intentions. What we are referring to is the position of many liberal churches and synagogues that appear to have no condemnatory attitude concerning the use of contraceptives. But a problem we see is that even these religions are giving confused moral statements by merely avoiding the issue of birth control or saying that it is permitted. Permissiveness is not the same as morality. One is tolerated and the other is a social good. We don't seem to give people enough opportunities to *practice* and think about morality. It seems to us that it should be taught, in those religions that permit the use of contraceptives, that it is a *moral act to use contraceptives* under certain conditions just as other religions may teach that it is an *immoral* act to use them. Both positions are correct relative to different religions, but if people are to make the wisest choices in all matters of sexual behavior, they have to practice moral decision making *after* the appropriate education in these matters, but long before the inevitable *choices*.

Let us now turn to our friends, the rabbi and the priest, and look at the traditional Judeo-Christian perspectives on birth control. First Rabbi Kravitz:

It would seem that from early times the Jews knew something about birth control. When the Rabbis read the Biblical story of Lamech and his two wives, Adah and Zillah, (Gen. 4:19) they suggested that one was for reproduction and the other for sex. The one for sex was given "a cup of roots," which made her barren. They also knew of some kind of sponge, a *mokh*, which

138

might prevent life—threatening situations affecting minors, pregnant women, and nursing mothers. That it might be used in situations that were other than life-threatening is suggested by their view that Esther used it at one point in her sexual relations with Ahasuerus.

That means of birth-control used by women might be licit follows from the assumption that the biblical commandment of *p'ru ur'vu* (Be fruitful and multiply) (Gen. 1:28) was given in the grammatically masculine form. However, many contemporary Orthodox rabbis would say that a woman is not to use birth control. They would say that having children is a *mitzvah*, a religious obligation, particularly at this time when there is a need to replenish the population of Jews murdered in the Holocaust. God, they feel, will somehow provide the resources to care for large families.

Among the Conservative and Reform branches of Judaism, birth control is not an issue. Even the use of condoms by males is accepted. However, for the orthodox, the male could not use a condom or any other means of birth control, such as *coitus interruptus*, because that would be the same as "spilling the seed."

Father Corr told us:

The traditional Roman Catholic view on birth control, just as with masturbation among married couples, stems from the fact of intention of the specific act. As we saw with masturbation, this could be complicated by the fact of masturbation being part of a process which culminates with the husband ejaculating inside his wife so that conception could take place. But with artificial birth control devices, the intention is clearly to avoid a pregnancy while at the same time enjoying the sexual act. This is still looked upon by most Catholics as a sin. It is not that one could not have family planning, since the church does allow for use of family planning methods such as the rhythm method, which permits avoiding conception through temporary abstinence during the fertile periods of the woman's menstrual cycle. But the use of chemical or barrier or other artificial methods would be considered by the church as "unnatural" as well as

139

thwarting the intent to permit the possibility of conception to take place.

When we asked our respondents about the use of birth control, they all seemed to be in agreement on one thing: Irrespective of what their religion may say, they, and their parents, favor the use of birth control within marriage (and for most, before marriage when the youth is sexually active). This was seldom placed in any moral context. Rarely, was any moral issue or even a traditional religious perspective expressed. Consider this from a young woman:

The only thing I ever heard about birth control was positive. You have to use it. If you're gonna do it, you gotta use it! It had nothing to do with religion. In my case, it wasn't that a Jew doesn't get pregnant before marriage, it was that "people don't." It was rarely stated, in any area of sex, that "Jews don't," it was always: "people don't." It was brought home to us that "good people" don't steal, "good people" don't take advantage of others and so forth.

This was a recurring theme that emerged as we explored most areas of sexual morality covered in this book with our respondents: The moral code that was taught, if any at all was communicated to them as children, was one that was oriented toward the people around them, and they were expected to measure up to some hypothetical ideal of what people do or don't do. It was rare to have anyone talk about some moral code based on religious values that provided explanation for why some behaviors were permitted and others were not. There was, for our respondents, almost never a matter of reasoning through why a behavior was right or wrong, moral or immoral.

For many of the people we talked with, despite their strong ties to their religion and church, birth control was a nonissue. For most religious persons we interviewed, other than Roman

140

Catholics, the kind of response presented by this young woman was typical:

> I really don't know if our church permits the use of birth con-
> trol or not. Armenian families aren't very large, usually only
> three or four children, so I don't think there is the same stress
> as in the Catholic church on procreation. I think, probably,
> birth control is O.K. in my church, according to what I've
> seen. I'm sure a lot of people do it, and I know it's not talked
> about.

The remarkable thing about this response is that this young woman is very much committed to her church and comes from a family that would be considered a traditional religious family. The impression we got from her is that she doesn't know what her church's position is and doesn't really care. This may seem an odd reaction from a person who seems to love her church, but as we learned more from her and others, it became more understandable. It was very much like the mothers we discussed in Chapter 5 whose method of handling information about their daughters' sexual activity is one of denial. If they don't know the daughter is having sex, they don't have to confront the reality—and peace and pretense of traditional morality is maintained. Knowledge may bring threatening confrontation. The same appears to be true about birth control for many who go to church and temple: Since they feel the need to practice birth control as a moral act inside of marriage, they believe it is better not to know their religion's rules on the matter. And it appears the ministers complement the parishioners' denial with their own avoidance of the issues. Rarely did any of our respondents, other than those belonging to the groups avowedly *opposed* to birth control, hear religious discussions of the morality of birth control in marriage from any source.

Some people who had attended parochial school recalled learning that artificial birth control was wrong, but it seemed to be more of a rote learning of a "right" answer than understanding why the behavior was wrong from their religion's moral perspective. It's like the parents who are proud of their child's religiosity and make the child recite the Ten Commandments in front of guests even though the child does not have the slightest understanding of the meaning of each Commandment. Such rote learning is reflected by this young woman:

It seems that I always knew that birth control was wrong, even when I didn't know what birth control was. I probably got this from the church or my family, but I didn't really know what birth control meant until I was 13 or 14. It seems that I knew that birth control was wrong before I knew how babies were made. In my marriage now, though, I practice birth control.

Another young woman told us that she never thought about birth control in terms of a moral issue because it was not an issue frequently discussed in Puerto Rico:

My mother told me, not too long ago, that she never realized that there was such a thing as birth control and that if she had known about it, she would only have had one child instead of four. Since I'm the oldest, I would have made it but not my brothers and sister. When I asked her why [she would have used birth control], she said that it was because she had the four children in about six years and couldn't do anything. If she had only one kid, she could have worked, moved out of this small town when times were bad and do other things. She didn't say what she used after the last kid to keep from getting pregnant again, but I know that my grandmother has always recommended sterilization with her in-laws. Each of them has been sterilized. Only the women, of course, never the men.

In general, there was little feeling or concern about birth control among the people we talked with. Some even seemed surprised to have it raised as an issue of morality. To most, it was simply a given fact of modern life: One uses birth control until one is ready to have a child. While some religious leaders may not accept the correctness of using artificial birth control, they must not ignore the tragedy of "children having children." We believe that these two issues are tied together. If the people we interviewed rarely, if ever, discussed the morality of using birth control devices with their families and religious associates, we can probably assume that teenagers who become pregnant also had very little discussion of birth control with their parents or religious associates. Common sense tells us that the discussion of the morality of using birth control devices cannot be separated from the discussion of the morality of engaging in premarital or nonmarital sex (and the inherent possibility of pregnancy). It seems that we may be more willing to sacrifice and often socially cripple young people with unwanted babies than to discuss the moral issues involved in making sexual choices. The parents who believe that "No!" satisfies their obligation to communicate moral values to their children are the people we must teach how to instill moral values and decision making in their own children within the context of their own religious commitment. This will not be an easy task.

143

CHAPTER 9

Abortion: Law versus Faith

No topic we discussed with our respondents elicited more emotional response, pro and con, than the subject of this chapter: abortion. It wasn't always *what* people said, but often *how* they said it—the tone of voice and, sometimes, the tension in their face. This is understandable because abortion always involves life-altering consequences no matter what frame of reference or perspective or belief system one brings to bear on the topic. For some, it is clearly and simply an issue of murdering the most helpless form of human life, the unborn child. For others, it is a viable and acceptable option to avoid having a child that may be seen as the ruination of their potential for a desired lifestyle and future career. And there are also those who see in the efforts to ban abortion an age-old reiteration of a male-dominated world that still wishes to impose controls and laws concerning what is going on inside of a woman's body. While we cannot examine this last perspective in this book because it lies outside the focus of sexual moral themes discussed by us, we should be aware that issues of sexual politics cannot be completely ignored in discussions on abortion as in other areas of sexuality. Abortion, more than any other sexual moral issue, demands that one should learn

145

the bases for moral decision making before having to make a choice and that impulsive choices are certainly to be avoided. Throughout history, and it seems in most cultures as well, strong views have been generated concerning the morality of abortion; yet surprisingly, there is no direct reference to abortion being moral or immoral in the Bible. Judeo-Christian views on abortion stem from definitions of when human life begins—an issue not directly addressed in the Bible. Thus, debates go on to the present—most often as a function of accepting one definition or another.

Ancient people seemed to accept abortion under certain social and physical conditions. Philosophers in ancient Greece had taken the position that abortion should be used to control family size or if the mother was too "old." In particular, Aristotle advocated that if a woman had more children than was appropriate, she should have an abortion before she felt the fetus moving within her, while Plato said that abortion should be obligatory for all women over the age of 40.[1]

Although the Bible does not talk directly about abortion or when life begins, later Jewish and Christian rejection of abortion seems to derive from a number of verses that imply that God symbolically creates life from dust or clay. A leading anthropologist and scholar of Middle Eastern studies, Raphael Patai, explains the biblical presentation of the origins of individual life in this way:

Thus man is clay and dust, not only in the historical sense, having descended from Adam whose body was fashioned by God from dust, but also in the more immediate sense of being made, individually and actually, of dust. . . . God fashions each human being of clay, as the potter fashions his pots (Isaiah 29:16; 45:9). "We are the clay and Thou our potter, and we all are the work of Thy hand" (Isaiah 64:7). The image of God as

---

[1] Guttmacher, Alan F., editor, *The Case for Legalized Abortion Now*, Berkeley: Diablo Press, 1967, p. 3.

the potter and man as the clay in His hands recurs in the New Testament as well (Romans 9:21).

At the same time, however, God also fashions man in the womb: . . . God fashions in the womb the master and the slave, the rich and the poor alike (Job 31:15; 34:19). . . .

The mystical component of the idea aside, it is clear from the passages quoted above that in the Biblical view the mother's body was regarded as merely a vessel in which the embryo is formed by God out of the seed of the father.[2]

Patai also points out that Job's reference to the process of his fetal development (Job 10:8-12) indicates the thinking of the time concerning the fetus:

The other [creative process], also the work of God, takes place in the mother's womb: it begins with a fluid state—perhaps a reference to the seminal fluid—then comes a process of coagulation, of jelling, the bones and sinews are formed and finally are clothed in flesh and skin.[3]

This appears to be the basis of one school of thought among some Jews that forbids abortion after the "coagulation," which some believe is indicated by movement of the fetus. Nevertheless, the ambiguity in the Bible of exactly when life or human life begins has resulted in somewhat different and complicated lines of thinking within Judaism and with much commentary in Jewish law on the subject—but with no absolute position or consensus of thought. Says Rabbi Kravitz:

Since Jewish Tradition did not view the fetus as a "soul," as an independent person, there was no difficulty in allowing abortion to save the life of the mother. Whether an abortion might be performed for other reasons, e.g., to avoid mental anguish for the mother, would become a matter of controversy. At present,

---

[2] Patai, Raphael. *Sex and Family in the Bible*, Garden City, N.Y.: Doubleday, 1959, pp. 182–183.

[3] *Ibid.*, p. 181.

most Conservative and Reform Rabbis would permit abortion on demand. Among present-day Orthodox Rabbis, there is some objection to abortion on demand, but all would agree to allowing abortion to preserve the life of the mother. It is my feeling that those who object to abortion on demand do so not because they view abortion as murder, but because they see in abortion on demand a threat to sexual morality, since it removes what might be considered to be the consequence of sexual immorality, an unwanted pregnancy.

Early Christianity also had mixed views on the permissibility of abortion, although they appear to have been very much against it. As late as the thirteenth century, St. Thomas Aquinas felt that life was indicated by knowledge and movement, supporting the proponents of the "quickening" theory of the beginning of human life. Many theologians had come to accept Aristotle's view that the development of the soul takes place in three stages: the vegetable soul at conception, then the animal soul and finally the higher rational or fully human soul. Aquinas maintained that quickening, or movement of the fetus, was an essential principle of rational or animated life, that is, the human soul. Following this reasoning, quickening marked the beginning of human life, indicating that the developmental process was complete—then believed to be forty days after conception for a male fetus and eighty days for a female.[4] Although, as historian Lawrence Lader has noted: "No one ever explained how fetal sex was to be determined."[5] The common law rule developed by the English jurist Bracton, a contemporary of Aquinas's, stated that life begins at the moment of quickening rather than a specific number of days after conception. Thus, in British common law of the time, abortion after quickening was murder, but before it was not. For the first time, abortion was placed under civil rather than ecclesiastic

---

[4] Lader, Lawrence. *Abortion*, Boston: Beacon Press, 1966, pp. 77–78.
[5] *Ibid.*, p. 77

law if it occurred after the fetus was animated.[6] Obviously, enforcement of this law was lax since only the mother's report of quickening could be practically valid.

In 1588, Pope Sixtus V declared all abortions would be considered murder, regardless of the number of days after conception they occurred, but the next pope, Gregory XIV, revoked all penalties except for abortions after forty days. Essentially, this lasted until 1869 when Pope Pius IX eliminated any distinction between animated and nonanimated fetuses and said that all abortions would be punished as murder.[7] As Father Corr told us, the position of the Roman Catholic church today is fundamentally still the same:

> The sin of abortion is the taking of human life which the church believes begins at conception. It is not the destruction of a soul which some people think because the soul cannot be killed. The soul will move on to eternity but the life is ended.

For the most part, abortion was not a criminal matter in the United States until early in the nineteenth century—the first abortion law came from Connecticut in 1821 but did not include abortion before quickening. For the next 150 years, laws were written and modified in the different states and most allowed for a medical abortion under approved conditions, only to save the life of the mother.

In the 1960s, a tranquilizer called thalidomide stirred up the foment concerning abortion. Mrs. Sherri Finkbine, hostess of a local children's television program, had taken thalidomide during the first few months of her fifth pregnancy. Later she learned that women in Europe who had taken this drug during the first trimester of their pregnancy often had deformed babies at birth: infants with flaps instead of arms, shortened

---

[6] *Ibid.*, p. 78.
[7] *Ibid.*, p. 79.

or no legs, missing ears, no arms and other birth defects. Her physician recommended a therapeutic abortion. Due to the publicity and legal issues, the hospital went to court to get a ruling on the abortion which it considered necessary but which the county attorney said was liable to prosecution. Because the court proceedings were likely to delay the abortion until it was too late, the Finkbines ultimately went to Sweden (after Japan had refused a visa because of the publicity). The abortion was performed—the fetus was deformed.[8]

Public sentiment began to mount for the removal of laws prohibiting abortion and stressing the right of a woman to control her body and not to continue a pregnancy if she and her physician deemed it harmful. Political and social action moved in the direction of limiting states' power to forbid abortion. The issue culminated in the landmark *Roe* v. *Wade* case in the United States Supreme Court in 1973 that challenged a Texas law prohibiting abortions except to save the woman's life. The Supreme Court held, in essence, that:

The [Texas] law is unconstitutional. The right to privacy extends to the decision of a woman in consultation with her physician to terminate her pregnancy. During the first trimester of pregnancy this decision may be effectuated free of state interference except a requirement that the abortion be performed by a licensed physician. After the first trimester, the state has a compelling interest in protecting the woman's health and may regulate abortion to promote that interest. At the point of fetal viability (capacity for sustained survival outside the uterus), the state has a compelling interest in protecting potential life and may proscribe abortion, except when necessary to preserve the woman's life or health.[9]

[8] Bullough, Vern L. *Sexual Variance in Society and History*, Chicago: The University of Chicago Press, 1976, pp. 657–658.
[9] Planned Parenthood Federation of America, Inc., Legal Division. "Major Supreme Court Reproductive Freedom Cases," from *Fact Sheet*, New York, 1986.

Ironically, the position of the Supreme Court in *Roe* v. *Wade* is not so very different from the older traditional religious view of Judaism and Catholicism.

The people we talked with often had strong and very eloquent statements to make about the morality of abortion and whether or not they had been taught about it from a moral perspective. From a young woman brought up in the Jewish Reform tradition but now unaffiliated:

> I think there is a Jewish perspective on abortion [that it is forbidden] if you are Orthodox, but for people like me, I think it is pro-choice. I really can't say what the Conservative or Reform position is merely because I have never in my life encountered a Conservative or Reform Jew who was against abortion or at least not pro-choice. If these faiths think that [opposition to abortion] is the belief the members are actually holding, then they are wrong because none of the participants I know of believe that.

And from another young woman where parental reaction is complex and based on a number of factors, but none directly related to the morality of abortion:

> I became pregnant at the age of 17 and after that my mother became very concerned about birth control since I chose to have an abortion. As soon as I became pregnant, I let my mother know. There was only a two-day period between the time I found out I was pregnant and going for the abortion. My mother was angry at me for not being more careful. I don't think she ever really wanted to know that I was having sex and this forced her to face that fact, so that this was probably another reason why she was upset. Now that this forced her to accept the fact that I was sexually active, this gave her a whole new bag of worries to be concerned with. Now she would have to worry about my getting a disease, about getting pregnant and so forth.

151

I felt bad about the abortion and cried. I didn't think that it was immoral but I felt bad about it. My mother didn't say it was immoral either, she was just very logical about it and said that pregnancy and having an abortion just was not a good thing for me to be doing at this time in my life—that I was too young. She never suggested that I speak to the rabbi about it. When she told my father about it some time later, he was very upset, but not so much that it happened but that I wouldn't tell him about it.

One young man told us the following lengthy story that shows how one deeply felt experience can create strong values and ethics concerning abortion—even when they contradict one's religious beliefs. We wish we could convey the power and emotional conviction that accompanied his story. Unfortunately, we can only recount the content:

The first time I ever had any strong feelings about abortion, one way or another, goes back to an incident I had when I was in college. I had read articles about abortion and remember talks about it in parochial school, but it never got home to me until one evening when I was serving as an auxiliary police officer while going to college. I was working out of one of the Manhattan precincts one very cold December night. My partner and I were standing on a street corner when we heard a woman screaming in Spanish at the top of her lungs for police. Fortunately, my partner was bilingual and understood her. While we were walking toward the apartment, my partner began to run and shout that a woman was bleeding to death in the apartment. We called for an ambulance on our walkie-talkie while we ran up. When we got upstairs, there was a rather messy situation. A young girl, about 17 years old, was lying in the bathtub with a clothes hanger hanging out of her vagina, blood running out of her. We gave her what first aid we could by raising her legs to ease the blood flow; an ambulance came in a few minutes and took her to the hospital.

We got the story of what happened from the older woman.

152

It seems that the younger girl was the niece of the older woman. She had been staying with her since coming up from Puerto Rico. She had met a young guy at a dance and had sex for the first time and as in many cases, the first time got her pregnant. This was just after the time that abortion became legal in the early 70s but for the Catholic background this girl came from it really wasn't accepted as "legal." Well this poor girl, she was with her aunt in New York, not close to her family, what was she to do? According to her aunt, she went to the local parish church, went to confession and got a real old time priest who was very insensitive and pulled out the unclean vessel doctrine of St. Paul and some other things. The bottom line was the girl was made to feel that she was a whore for doing this, and she felt that she had to get rid of the baby without anyone knowing about it. So she did the old coat hanger trick and managed to perforate her uterus.

Yes, she lived but according to the precinct who did a follow-up on her, she also had to have her uterus taken out and it was a fairly touch-and-go situation for about four or five days.

We reminded him of what he had told us earlier about his religious and parochial school upbringing; about what he had heard in the church and school concerning abortion being murder—but none of it had as profound an effect on him as this one incident:

This really affected me because—I was brought up on the Lower East Side of Manhattan and we had heard the rumors about the abortion mills there in the tenements. Every once in a while when they ripped down an old tenement, we used to hear about a couple of fetuses being buried in the dirt floor of the tenement or in the walls. Basically, I came to the conclusion after that incident with the girl that if a woman is determined to have an abortion, she is going to have an abortion. And, if she is going to have an abortion, you might as well make it as safe for her as you possibly can.

153

We asked him how he could maintain this position even though the cardinal and the church hierarchy does not agree with him and would say that his position is morally wrong:

Yes, I still believe this. Let me put it this way: I'm a Catholic. I was born a Catholic. But, I don't have the right to impose my morality on somebody else. I don't have the right to impose my morality on you because I am a Catholic and you are a Jew. It's just like I don't have the right to tell you who you should or shouldn't go to bed with or what God you are supposed to pray to.

Religious families may have conflicting views among each other as well as from their church. From a young woman:

My father is opposed to abortion and he thinks that it is murder. But my mother, to my surprise, does not agree with him because she thinks that at times it is the only thing a woman can do. They would both be opposed to abortion before marriage [probably because it would also imply an acceptance of premarital sex].

Other respondents, who were also religious and committed to their church, disagreed on the issue of abortion for other reasons. From a young woman who had been influenced as a child to consider becoming a nun:

I don't think that a priest or a nun could influence me today to become a nun, because when they talk to you about abortion and things like that, I say: "No [you're wrong about abortion]," because I'm very political. . . . I know what I consider good for the whole people [Caribbean Hispanics], so when they come along, I say: "Sorry, I don't believe that." If a woman wants an abortion, it's up to her; I don't care what the pope says. I know it sounds funny for a person who goes to church every Sunday,

154

but that's how I feel. Yes, I take communion, but I still feel that I am at peace with God.

As we said earlier, no topic concerning sexual issues causes more emotional conflict and anguish than abortion—not even homosexuality. But, unlike homosexuality, abortion is primarily a matter of choice. The legalization of abortion via the Supreme Court or any other state legislative body does not make abortion right or moral; it simply removes the state criminal justice apparatus from something that is fundamentally a moral and medical issue. This is a position we support. There are some who would say that the morality of abortion is directly a function of different theological definitions on the beginning of human life. To a large extent this is true. But, what happens when moral issues conflict with less clear moral issues such as pregnancy by forced incest of a child, or rape, or mentally disturbed young women who would hate their child even before it is born and destroy it soon after? And, what of the young women who are not committed to any particular religion? If the definition of the beginning of human life is essentially theological, should they be free of censure while their religious sisters be punished? Or, are we to make what is essentially a religious tenet part of our criminal justice apparatus once again as we did hundreds of years ago? Unfortunately, there is little consensus either in the medical or the theological fields. We know that we have the tendency to oversimplify very compli-cated moral issues in this book. This is deliberate. The people who must make everyday moral decisions are rarely steeped in comparative theology, or even the theology of their own religion. On the other hand, the alternative to a degree in theology is not blind obedience without any understanding. The moral issue in abortion rests not only on an acceptance of the beginning of human life but also on other moral issues involved in any specific situation. Once human life begins, the willful taking of it would be wrong from almost any religious perspective, if we ignore all other moral considerations, and it

155

could even be considered murder (or foeticide in Jewish law).* Rarely, however, is abortion considered apart from any other moral consideration. But, even then, does *human* life begin at the instant of conception? Or at the quickening? Or at the end of the second trimester? Or when the fetus is viable without artificial life support? Or at the emergence of the head when the "breath of life" is taken? We cannot answer this question for you. On one hand, it is a matter of faith; on the other, a matter of scientific debate. If science cannot provide the answer, then one must rely on faith—the faith of one's own religious commitment—and then be morally responsible for one's own choices.

---

* We are deliberately avoiding the subject of terminating a fetus that may be, for example, grossly deformed or incapable of life outside the womb since these situations also involve the very complicated and controversial issue of euthanasia. Although this is also a very important moral issue, it is not a sexual moral issue and cannot be viewed as a clear issue of abortion choice. Thus, it is outside the scope of this book; but as we strive for more training in moral literacy in general, such issues must not be forgotten.

156

CHAPTER 10

Oral Sex–Anal Sex:
From Perversion
to Diversion

When we were growing up in the 1930s and 1940s, sex was not discussed openly in "polite circles" and mixed company. Even on those rare occasions when we did discuss sex with our peers, there seemed to have been a simple dichotomy between behavior that was considered "normal" (the "missionary" sexual position of husband on top of wife) and everything else that many children (and adults) called "immoral," "abnormal," "deviant" or "perverted". Many of us knew that homosexuals engaged in oral and anal sex (and therefore thought it was abnormal because it was homosexual), but there were many arguments about oral and anal sex between husbands and wives. Would this too be considered "abnormal" or "perverted"? Since it was unlikely that we could ever have gone to an adult for such answers (what would adults have known about sex anyway?), we could only speculate and often resort to the sexual attitudes of the nineteenth century that had lasted long into the twentieth century. Fallacious beliefs such as that oral and anal sex could cause cancer and other devastating diseases were widely accepted (the very real danger of AIDS was, of course, not known at the time). One account of these mistaken views

157

is reported by the historian Vern L. Bullough in his book *Sexual Variance in Society and History*:

> One [late nineteenth century sex] manual reported the case history of a young woman whose husband "had the fatal habit of applying the tongue and lips to his wife's genitals to provoke in her a venereal orgasm." The unavoidable result was "gastralgia" [stomach pains] and "constant exhaustion" in the woman, until the physician treating her felt called upon to warn her that her very life would be in danger unless her husband ceased this foul practice. The physician warned that cunnilingus [oral stimulation of the vulva or clitoris] and fellatio [oral stimulation of the penis] would cause a cancer of the tongue, and anal intercourse would result in even greater afflictions. The worst danger of all was that if anyone engaging in such "perversions" had offspring, the child itself would be born with perverted instincts.[1]

Although we may find such reasoning farfetched and even amusing, the reality of AIDS is not amusing and forces us to bring realistic medical considerations back into discussions of oral and anal sex. Nonetheless, we should not confuse moral considerations with medical concerns, and we will try to keep these issues separate as we proceed through this chapter. As you will find, this chapter is shorter than most, mainly because so few of the people we talked with had ever even considered oral and anal sex as either moral or immoral. For most of them, it was a non-issue—just another way of enhancing sexual expressions between two people. Let us first examine some of the cultural and historical factors that may shed some light on the current attitudes (or non-attitudes).

In many cultural traditions and religions, oral and anal sex were permitted and even encouraged. In India, for example, although some leaders of the Hindu religion were officially

---

[1] Bullough, Vern L. *Sexual Variance in Society and History*. New York: John Wiley, 1976, p. 547.

disapproving of oral-genital contact, the erotic manuals present at the time discussed it at length and gave specific instructions as to how it was to be performed.[2] Similarly, in these erotic manuals from about the eleventh and twelfth centuries A.D., there appeared to be an openness about the erotic value in lovemaking that involved many parts of the body:

> The handbooks emphasize that sexual desire in women depends on several things, including . . . stimuli. . . . This last is regarded as under the male's control; he is supposed to acquire a thorough knowledge of woman's erogenous zones—the breasts, nipples, nape of the neck, folds of the buttocks, labia and clitoris. . . . The . . . [erogenous zone] most frequently praised in the Sanskrit literature . . . [is] . . . the female pudenda, including the buttocks and the anus . . . which was regarded as a particular area of delight. Graphic descriptions of the rear parts of various legendary beauties are found in the classics as well as the various vernaculars.[3]

For a much more extensive accounting of this tradition and sexual behavior in other cultural traditions of Western, Eastern and ancient civilizations, including China, India, Islam and Africa, we recommend the excellent historical work by Bullough, which we consider to be the finest study of variances in sexual behaviors in different cultures available today.

As for the biblical Jews and early Christians, there are no clear references concerning oral and anal sex in either the Old or the New Testament, although perhaps some inferences can be made in reference to *homosexual* contacts—but this appears to have applied only to men having sex with men. (We will discuss the biblical statements on homosexuality in the next chapter.) Early Christian attitudes regarding the moral desirability or even permissibility for married heterosexuals to engage in either oral or anal sex were not clear until the fifth

---

[2] *Ibid.*, pp. 261–263.
[3] *Ibid.*, p. 252.

century when St. Augustine provided a definition of what was "unnatural" in human sexual behavior. Essentially, it was based on the principle that sexual intercourse in marriage was good providing it led to conception. As Bullough has noted:

> Anything else [related to sexual activities other than the use of the penis for the process of ejaculation into the vagina] went beyond the natural use, which he defined as using a member [sexual organ] not granted for this purpose [conception]. [St. Augustine's] . . . definition [of "unnatural" sexual behavior], then, would include using contraceptives of any kind, engaging in anal intercourse, masturbation, homosexual activity, coitus interruptus, bestiality, oral-genital contacts, and, in effect, anything not leading to conception. Augustine established the intellectual basis for the belief in a sin against nature that much later entered the law codes as the crime against nature.[4]

Many of the religious discussions and writings before and after St. Augustine focussed on the sinful behavior of the people of Sodom, described in the Old Testament (Genesis 19:4-8). While rape was also one of the sins mentioned in the account, over the centuries the word "sodomy" began to become a synonym for homosexuality—a sexual behavior also implied in the story of Sodom. Since homosexuals frequently engage in anal and oral sex, sodomy eventually became a catch-all term for these behaviors even when engaged in by heterosexual couples.

From the time of the settlement of the American colonies through the nineteenth and early twentieth centuries, criminal laws against sodomy (the term that was generally used) existed in all states. Generally, sodomy and "crimes against nature" meant the same thing, and it was up to the legal authorities in the specific jurisdictions to determine if a known sexual act came under these laws. For the most part, these laws appeared

---

[4]*Ibid.*, p. 355.

to have been unenforceable because the behaviors were generally private and consensual. Laws against sodomy, which included both oral and anal sex, seemed aimed primarily against homosexuals rather than heterosexuals.

In the 1940s, the Kinsey study found that people had become more tolerant of various private heterosexual activities, particularly between husband and wife (among unmarried people, such activities were more accepted for males than females).[5] As laws concerning consensual sexual acts were gradually eliminated from state penal codes, these behaviors eventually became almost a non-issue. But, as we said earlier in this chapter, now the problem of AIDS has changed things. Anal sex seems to be the most common way to sexually transmit AIDS from an infected person to someone else. Thus, although anal sex may no longer be a legal issue, it cannot remain a *non*-issue. It has become a serious concern to the medical profession and should be a serious concern to everyone who engages in it. At this time, we don't know whether there are the same risks in oral-genital sex, but research continues to be done in the hope of finding better answers in the near future.

The Judeo-Christian tradition appears to have no clear *moral* position on either oral or anal sex among married heterosexuals, except as part of the broad category of sexual behavior that could not result in procreation. It appears that neither of these behaviors when practiced between husband and wife are of much concern to either Jewish or Christian theologians and religious commentators (outside of marriage they would, of course, be forbidden). But as Rabbi Kravitz told us, they probably would not be accepted among the Orthodox today. There is a basic Jewish principle governing all marital sexual activity that bans the use of a spouse's body for solely one's own pleasure without a mutuality of desire and commitment. Thus, it would not be condoned if one partner imposed or

---

[5] Kinsey, Alfred C., W. Pomeroy and C. Martin. *Sexual Behavior in the Human Female,* Philadelphia: W. B. Saunders, 1948, pp. 369–371.

161

insisted on engaging in either sexual act, but if both partners in the marriage find it pleasurable, it would not be forbidden. Father Corr stated the Catholic position as follows:

The attitude of a large portion of the official church today is, just as I indicated with masturbation, that oral sex and even anal sex may not be a sin if the intention of the husband and wife is for it to be part of a process ending with normal ejaculation so that there is the possibility of the creation of a new life. Otherwise, these acts would be sins. And certainly, outside of marriage they are not permitted. Intention, therefore, is, in this case, to be taken into consideration in order to determine if the oral and anal sex play is sinful or not.

And for the Protestants? As in all the other sexual areas we have discussed, there is such a considerable variety of interpretations and considerations that one would have to go to the specific denomination or group and discuss the issue with the minister to learn their perspective.

As we said earlier in this chapter, few of the people we interviewed had much to say about the moral issues of oral and anal sex. The most typical response we heard from our respondents was "I can't ever remember hearing about either."

Not too much moral instruction there! For some, who came from traditional or more rigorous religious backgrounds, there may have been some attempt in parochial school to discuss these matters, as this young man tells us:

In a health class [in the parochial high school] what they said about anal sex was that it was considered to be a deviancy. Basically, if you do it, you're a deviant, you're a "sicko" in the head. He [the brother] said that homosexuals do it and sometimes heterosexuals do it, very little more was said. Nothing was mentioned about the moral issues because of the framework in which the course was taught. We were told that this was a course required by the State Board of Regents, with state funding, and they weren't supposed to bring in the moral aspects. Even though it was taught by a brother in a cassock, he kept to the rules. There was another brother in another class who said that this is wrong, it is against God's law and so forth, but my teacher said that he would not talk about morality because he didn't want to jeopardize the funding.

It seems to us that maybe something is wrong when we try to teach sexuality without reference to morality. At best, it becomes confusing. As we have said repeatedly and will say more about in our concluding chapter, a firm moral under-standing of one's own religious bases for sexual standards is necessary for making appropriate choices. The teacher who labels people who engage in oral or anal sex as "deviant" or "sicko" underscores the necessity for people who teach sex education to receive appropriate and modern education *before* they are let loose possibly to harm young and sensitive minds. From a young woman who also was deprived of appropriate moral and sex education in this area:

> I definitely did not learn anything about oral sex, right or wrong or anything, from my parents or from the church. I don't remember anybody sitting me down and talking to me about oral sex. The first time I heard about it was from my friends, when I was in my teens. I remember that the first time I heard about it I was repulsed by the thought of it. I didn't know that people did that. I think that the church would think that it is dirty because all they believe in is the missionary position. The same thing about anal sex. I never heard about it from my family or the church. It was my boyfriend who taught me about it.

From a young woman around 20 whose parents never talked to her about *any* sexual matters, behavioral or moral:

> Although I knew that people had oral sex, I never really knew what it was until I was in college and saw pictures in a human sexuality textbook. I brought the books from the course home,

163

but I hid them because I didn't want my younger sisters to see them. It wasn't that I was afraid that they would tell my mother, but that they would ask me questions and talk to me. And I don't want to talk to them about sex. I feel it really is my responsibility to talk to them about sex since my parents don't, but I feel very uncomfortable about it.

When parents hope and try to keep their children ignorant of sexual knowledge, they should be aware that they are also helping to keep them ignorant about sexual morality. This is because it is almost impossible to sensibly communicate a moral position concerning sexual behavior without some knowledge of what is being discussed. This amusing story from a young Puerto Rican woman shows parental unwillingness to discuss sexual issues with children:

I never heard anybody discussing oral or anal sex, except for one incident. I was in the living room with my mother and some friends of hers when I was a teenager, and they were very angry at this woman. They called her something which would be loosely translated into English as a "trumpet player." My mother saw me there, and she became very uncomfortable when she realized that I had heard that. They changed the subject very quickly. I didn't know until much later that it referred to oral sex.

From a young woman about 35 who had negative views, moral and otherwise, presented to her by her mother:

Yes, my mother did tell me that oral sex was wrong. I was in high school then and I had just heard about oral sex and mentioned it to her. She thought that it was terrible, that it was totally wrong, and I could tell that she found the whole concept sort of disgusting. She didn't tell me that it was wrong from a religious point of view or from a health perspective only that she found it repulsive. No, no one in Bible class or elsewhere ever mentioned oral sex. No one ever mentioned anal sex either.

164

In Bible class when we learned about Sodom, no one ever explained that there was any connection between Sodom and the word "sodomy"—only that something bad happened at Sodom, but no details. These were very nonphysical people in Bible camp, and they didn't like to talk about anything related to the physical body. I had no idea that anal sex even existed until I became friends with some homosexuals in high school. By then, I had gotten a pretty liberal education from my friends and was pretty much of a libertine since I was being told from them that anything was O.K.

The last comment by this woman raises another issue: the medical concern about the transmission of AIDS, especially where nonmarital sexual behavior is concerned. The rule that "anything goes" in sexual behavior as long as it is consensual may have been somewhat fashionable during the 1960s and 1970s, but it cannot be an acceptable code today. Since this book is primarily concerned with the moral questions related to sexual behavior, we do not examine the possible medical consequences of behaviors such as oral and anal sex. On the other hand, as practitioners and concerned human beings, it would be immoral for us to ignore the severe medical implications that do exist; our repeated references to the dangers attest to our awareness and concern. For those readers who have not already done so, we emphatically suggest that they get a good, up-to-date sex manual or speak to a physician about the possible health hazards of oral and anal sex when one or the other partner has an illness. This is particularly essential in light of the AIDS problem.

The brevity of this chapter indicates that oral or anal sex within marriage is not a moral issue of great concern to most people—it has become, as we suggest in the title of this chapter, a diversion to enhance the sexual life of the spouses. If anything negative was mentioned, it only concerned aesthetics and physical discomfort rather than morality. Oral and anal sex outside of marriage raise the same moral issues for most persons as does intercourse. There are some persons we have heard of (but have not run across) who believe that the loss of virginity for the woman is a more immoral act than oral sex, and so they would engage in that while remaining "technical virgins." We find very little support for this view among those concerned with moral issues.

Our many interviews with people revealed that discussions and training in sexual morality decision making rarely preceded sexual knowledge. If any sexual morality was taught, it usually came long after sexual knowledge and often long after sexual experimentation and activity. With respect to oral and anal sex, it seems that virtually no communications were given to our respondents when they were young, not even simple prohibition similar to what we described in the chapters on masturbation, nudity and nonmarital sex. Is this because oral and anal sex are not considered to be moral issues separate from the issues involved in nonmarital sex? Is it because parents and others cannot imagine that their teenagers are engaging in these activities? Or is it because parents, educators and the religious are uncomfortable discussing these subjects with young persons? We cannot answer these questions. But we can say that moral training in these sexual behaviors (as in all others) must be accompanied by discussion and good education in the physical aspects of sexuality.

Finally, we must warn that the moral issues of anal and oral sex must not be confused with the medical issues and fear of AIDS. The medical realities are indisputable and universal, the moral issues are unique to specific religions and individuals and must satisfy the beliefs and needs of those who follow them.

CHAPTER 11

Homosexuality:
A Moral Dilemma

With the exception of abortion, homosexuality probably causes more emotional response and concern among lay persons than any of the other issues addressed in this book. Our impression is that while abortion is more of a concern to religious leaders and ministers than to the laity, homosexuality engenders very strong emotional responses, both pro and con, from most people. And now that AIDS is of major concern, the questions and morality issues connected with homosexuality are even more salient.

We called this chapter "Homosexuality: A Moral Dilemma" because it is the only issue we cover where there is considerable doubt whether appropriate and wise *choices* are available for people who engage in homosexual activity. Whereas heterosexuals may choose to engage in nonmarital sex or choose to wait until the right partner comes along for a socially and/or religiously sanctioned marriage, homosexuals cannot choose to wait for a socially and/or religiously sanctioned marriage because there is none at the present time. In this way, their right to choose is denied. As we will see, they did not *choose* to become homosexuals and they cannot *choose* to limit their sexual expression to a socially and/or religiously sanctioned

167

relationship. The only way in which they might have the same moral choices as heterosexuals would be for traditional moral belief systems to change so that the homosexual expression of love would be considered as moral as the heterosexual. We will see that this is no easy task.

As children and young adults, many of us encountered three contradictory positions regarding homosexuality, all of which still occasion much debate and controversy:

- The homosexual got that way because he or she chose to engage in such activities when young and grew to like it.
- The homosexual got that way because he or she is emotionally disturbed with the roots of that disturbance amenable to analysis and thus psychiatric treatment.
- The homosexual orientation of a person is determined long before social and emotional learning takes place, perhaps genetically or in utero.

While a review of the literature does not conclusively prove any one explanation, the research in this field in recent years has led us to accept the last of the three propositions: The homosexual no more *chooses* homosexuality than the heterosexual *chooses* heterosexuality. One can no more *cause* someone to become a homosexual than *cause* someone to become a heterosexual. Homosexuality is no more of an emotional disorder than heterosexuality is an emotional disorder. But the Bible says homosexuality is wrong—and that is at the crux of the moral dilemma.

Now that you know where we stand on the issue, let us look at the subject in the same manner we approached the other issues, because we believe very strongly that moral education in this area is as vital as in all other matters.

The existence of homosexuality since the earliest days of our history is evident from the literature and artifacts of ancient civilizations. Homosexuality has been noted in many cultures throughout the world, and in some it was so acceptable that men who did not engage in homosexual activity may have been considered abnormal.[1] Obviously, these men were not exclusively homosexual or the society would not have been able to reproduce itself. Were they homosexuals who chose heterosexual acts for reproduction only, or were they heterosexuals who chose homosexual acts for whatever reason? In either case, doesn't this contradict what we said earlier as to the likelihood that one is "born" a homosexual? Not necessarily, because there is another concept that complicates discussions of homosexuality—bisexuality.

A popular belief is that one is either a heterosexual or a homosexual and that one is classified as one or the other depending on whether one engages in sex with people of the opposite sex or of the same sex. It is not so simple. There are many people who engage in sex with people of both sexes. Others are sexually attracted to both sexes but either choose to stay with only one partner (who may be of the same or opposite sex) or to refrain from having any sex (perhaps because the choice is too hard). Society will label some of these people as heterosexuals and some as homosexuals—in reality, they are bisexuals. Confusing, we know, but it is necessary to know this to discuss the subject of homosexuality. The major statement concerning this range of hetero-homo-sexual behavior was presented by Alfred Kinsey back in 1948:

> The histories which have been available in the present study make it apparent that the heterosexuality or homosexuality of many individuals is not an all-or-none proposition. It is true that there are persons in the population whose histories are exclusively heterosexual, both in regard to their overt experience and in regard to their psychic reactions. And there are individuals in the population whose histories are exclusively homosexual, both in experience and in psychic reactions. But the record also shows that there is a considerable portion of the population

---

[1] Ford, Clellan S. "Culture and Sex," *The Encyclopedia of Sexual Behavior*, Albert Ellis and Albert Abarbanel, editors, vol. 1, New York: Hawthorn Books, 1961, p. 308.

whose members have combined, within their individual histories, both homosexual and heterosexual experiences and/or psychic responses. . . . For instance, there are some who engage in both · heterosexual and homosexual activities in the same year, or in the same month or week, or even the same day.[2]

Kinsey and his associates then went on to make this now classic comment on human sexual behavior:

Males do not represent two discrete populations, heterosexual and homosexual. The world is not to be divided into sheep and goats. Not all things are black nor all things white. It is a fundamental of taxonomy that nature rarely deals with discrete categories. Only the human mind invents categories and tries to force facts into separated pigeon-holes. The living world is a continuum in each and every one of its aspects. The sooner we learn this concerning human sexual behavior the sooner we shall reach a sound understanding of the realities of sex.[3]

Kinsey devised a seven-point heterosexual-homosexual rating scale that he used to rate a sample of 4,275 males aged 16–55. After analyzing the results in many ways, he reached a number of conclusions including this one about bisexuality:

Since only 50 percent of the [total male, married and single] population is exclusively heterosexual throughout its adult life, and since only 4 percent of the population is exclusively homosexual throughout its life, it appears that nearly half (46%) of the population engages in both heterosexual and homosexual activities, or reacts to persons of both sexes, in the course of their adult lives.[4]

---

[2] Kinsey, Alfred C., W. Pomeroy and C. Martin. *Sexual Behavior in the Human Male*, Philadelphia: W. B. Saunders, 1948, p. 639.
[3] *Ibid.*, p. 639.
[4] *Ibid.*, p. 656.

Why do we emphasize the pespective and findings of Kinsey? It is to caution the reader that many discussions and pronouncements in the past and present concerning homosexuality seem to be based on dubious logic and misconceptions. Let us erase some of these misconceptions. First, engaging in a homosexual act does not necessarily mean someone is a homosexual. Many adults, male and female, experiment with homosexual acts out of curiosity or engage in homosexual acts because of the unavailability of partners of the opposite sex, but they still prefer—and are primarily attracted to—people of the opposite sex. Second, many, if not most, children and teenagers, girls as well as boys, will engage in homosexual activity as part of the growing process of their self identity, but are not likely to develop a homosexual sex preference. Some will, but most will not. Finally, as evidenced by their frequency and the growing acceptance by psychologists and psychiatrists that homosexuality is not an emotional disorder, homosexual acts—even when engaged in by persons who are basically heterosexual—should not be considered "abnormal" human behavior. We are not trying to suggest that just *because* large numbers of persons may engage in homosexual acts, it is somehow "right" or acceptable. After all, even though most people lie at least on occasion, such behavior is not "right" or acceptable. On the other hand, such an analogy is not entirely valid because lying is almost always a matter of choice, whereas one doesn't choose to become a homosexual.

We believe that much of the confusion results from the fact that most people are not aware of what Kinsey had documented so carefully four decades ago: Some people who are basically heterosexual may choose for capricious or other reasons to engage in a homosexual act, but they are not what we would recognize today as "homosexuals." The homosexual whom most people seem to be concerned about today is the one whose lifestyle is predominantly homosexual, whose affection and attraction and sexual identity is predominantly homosexual, the one who is not making a sexual political statement or a

171

hedonistic capricious choice but who feels completely that he or she is homosexual. Homosexuals know that they cannot change their sex preference, just as heterosexuals know that they cannot change their sex preference.

So where does this leave us? Some things are clear: Homosexual acts in the total population are quite widespread, more so than is commonly assumed. While for some, a specific homosexual act may be entered into out of choice, this appears to be not so for the population of "gay" persons about whom there has been so much controversy. These people appear to be expressing their sexual nature not contradicting it. Given these facts, however, it is still not clear whether a specific homosexual act or a homosexual identity is morally "right" or "wrong." Let us see what history tells us about this dilemma.

The ancient Greeks, including Plato, seemed very tolerant of male homosexuality, almost to the point of idealizing it.[5] Male homosexuality was also accepted in Roman culture as a natural part of man's sensual life, although it does not appear to have been as deeply ingrained in the culture as in Greece— nor did the Romans appear to have the same fascination with homosexuality and sensuality among youth as did the Greeks.[6] But biblical law for the Jews is unequivocal and very punitive: "Thou shalt not lie with mankind, as with womankind; it is abomination." (Leviticus 18:22) "And if a man lie with mankind, as with womankind, both of them have committed abomination: they shall surely be put to death; their blood shall be upon them." (Leviticus 20:13) Curiously, no mention is made of females "lying" with females. Of this, the anthropologist Raphael Patai says:

It is remarkable that while both men and women are warned against the practice of bestiality, no reference at all is made to

---

[5] Bullough, Vern L. *Sexual Variance in Society and History*, Chicago: The University of Chicago Press, 1976, pp. 100–105.
[6] Wood, Robert. "Sex Life in Ancient Civilization," in Ford, pp. 125–130.

female homosexuality in the Levitical law, nor anywhere else in the Bible. Although female homosexuality must have existed among the ancient Hebrews just as it did in Greece and as it still does in the Middle East today, it seems that either it was regarded as a matter of no consequence, or—being an affair of women among themselves—little notice of it was taken by men.[7]

But on the same page, Patai cautions the reader that "careful distinction must be made between the legal position and folk mores." he goes on to point out that:

As opposed to the law, in actual practice male homosexuality was rampant in Biblical times and has so remained in the Middle East down to the present day. It may not have been as general as it was in ancient Greece, but the folk mores certainly did not regard it with any measure of disapproval.[8]

There are similar incidents in two biblical stories, one involving Sodom (Genesis 19:4–8) and the other Gibeah (Judges 19:22–26). In both, a mob of men comes to someone's house and demands the male guest (or two angels in Sodom) to come out so that they can have sex together. Each master refuses to send his guest(s) out of his house but offers the mob one or two women instead. Patai comments on these biblical incidents:

. . . there is no reason to suppose that the mores of these two localities were greatly different from those of the other Canaanite and Israelite towns and villages. Even the authors of the passages describing the incidents in Sodom and Gibeah, who lived in later days when individuals with a stricter morality may have regarded the practice with abhorrence, have not a word of condemnation for homosexuality per se. What they condemn and execrate is the intended violation by the Sodomite and Gibeahite mobs of the visiting strangers. This would have been

---

[7] Patai, Raphael. *Sex and Family in the Bible and the Middle East*, New York: Doubleday, 1959, p. 168.
[8] *Ibid.*, p. 169.

rape and, as such, just as sinful as the rape of a woman, and, in fact, worse, because it would have been also a flagrant violation of the sacred institution of hospitality.[9]

As Patai tells us, the stories are condemning of cruel *people* and the cruel act of forcing oneself upon others, whether male or female, but not condemning of the homosexual acts. If there was very little condemnation of homosexual acts, why was there such a strong law forbidding it? An intriguing explanation was suggested by Dr. William Graham Cole, formerly professor of religion at Williams College:

> Homosexuality was to them [the Hebrews and the early church] a sin and a crime, and that attitude has entered deeply into the texture of Western civilization. Why they should have reacted so violently to a practice obviously confined to a negligible part of the population is not clear. The early Hebrews struggled against a cruel nature and the threats of other nomadic tribes. Could it be that their population policy required that all sexual activity be directed to procreation? This would represent a kind of economic determinism, and there may be some truth in it. A somewhat more plausible theory, more plausible because there is some evidence for it in the Old Testament itself, traces the objection to homosexuality to religious roots. Israel's pagan neighbors in the Fertile Crescent used male cult prostitutes in their exaltation of sexuality as the creative principle in nature. This would associate homosexuality with idolatry in the minds of the religious leaders in the Hebrew nation and would be sufficient to condemn the custom.[10]

The New Testament has similarly strict references to homosexuality, and it is condemned as one of the sins (I Corinthians 6:9; Romans 1:27). Although Jesus did not speak about homosexuality, the apostle Paul referred to it in very negative terms

---

[9] *Ibid.*
[10] Cole, William Graham. *Sex and Love in the Bible*, New York: Association Press, 1959, p. 343.

at several points. Cole points out that in one lengthy passage (Romans 1:18–28):

[Paul] . . . traced homosexuality to idolatry, to the failure to know God. . . . A false understanding of God leads to a distorted understanding of one's self and his proper role. . . . Confusion in one leads inevitably to confusion in the other.[11]

Again, the assumption behind the reasoning of St. Paul, as interpreted by Cole, seems to be that the cause and thus the "cure" for homosexuality lies in the freedom of choice of homosexuals not to be homosexuals. If Paul was wrong and homosexuals *cannot* choose (as we believe today), this is a tragic dilemma indeed!

Some religious leaders are clearly disturbed by the issue but may feel that their hands are tied by their own belief. For example, this is what the television Evangelical minister Dr. Robert E. Schuller of the Crystal Cathedral told us he suggests:

I stand squarely in the traditional moral sexual position. I do not approve, and our church does not approve, sexual activity outside of a loving, bonded commitment, and the only loving, bonded commitment that we recognize is marriage. This would include not only male with female but also of male with male. Since the Bible is our source of authority, we cannot find in either the Old or New Testaments a basis for the approval of marriage between people of the same sex. This means that when people join our church—I don't know if they are heterosexual or homosexual and it doesn't make any difference—I say: "You can be a member in good and regular standing in this church whatever your sexual orientation is, as long as you do not practice sex outside the bonds of marriage."

We do have people in this church who have come to me and said: "Dr. Schuller, I'm gay, I'm homosexual, can I belong to the church?" And, they are quick to say: "But, I do not practice

---

[11] *Ibid.*, pp. 361–362.

sexuality, I'm celibate, I masturbate, but I do not practice sex with another human being." That's fine. We have no problem with his masturbating to relieve sexual pressures.

Other ministers believe that it is not sufficient to rely solely on past interpretations of scripture. For example, Reverend Foster McCurley of the Lutheran church and a member of its task force on homosexuality was quoted in a recent article by Edward Tivnan in the *New York Times Magazine*: "In the final analysis . . . the Bible does not relieve us of the awesome responsibility to search for theological truth and for pastoral care to all persons."[12]

Others have taken even stronger positions. In a report on family life and sexuality, the Episcopal Diocese of Newark, New Jersey, headed by Bishop John S. Spong, suggested ways of bringing homosexuals into full acceptance by the church:

> "The church," said the report, "must learn how to continue to affirm the conventional without denigrating alternative sexual and family arrangements. . . . The church must find ways genuinely to affirm persons as they faithfully and responsibly choose and live out other modes of relationship." The diocese has agreed to study a proposal allowing priests to bless homosexual "marriages."[13]

A conference of 150 members of the clergy and 360 lay delegates of the Newark diocese, together representing 125 churches in northern New Jersey, voted to accept the proposal. According to Bishop Spong, the group voted only to *bless* nontraditional unions such as a homosexual couple (or a heterosexual couple living outside of marriage) but not to perform gay "marriages" (that is, to recognize these unions

[12]Tivnan, Edward. "Homosexuals and the Churches," *New York Times Magazine*, October 11, 1987, p. 89.
[13]*Ibid.*, p. 91.

within the church but not to carry out marriage ceremonies for gay couples).[14]

When we interviewed Bishop Spong recently, he told us that his new book, *Living in Sin? A Bishop Rethinks Human Sexuality*, concerns issues of nontraditional unions, premarital sexual unions, postmarital sexual unions (usually of older persons), and homosexual unions.[15] Since these sexual lifestyles are not ordinarily blessed by the Episcopal church (or any other religion we know of), he analyzes the scriptural and historical bases of accepting and rejecting different sexual lifestyles in the context of the historical and cultural forces at different times in history. His objective is to find a religious basis so that couples, heterosexual or homosexual, in these relationships may come into the church and have their relationship, in an accepting and loving manner, blessed within the church.

Where will the religious debate end? No one can be sure. But of one thing we can be sure, the status quo, which is based upon traditional interpretation, does not seem to provide a satisfactory solution for our times.

And what of our respondents? What had they been told? One would assume that if most parents (wrongly) believe that one becomes a homosexual by choice, there would be considerable moral teaching about the subject. Not so. Very few of our respondents had anything to say about the subject. Most "knew" that their religion believed it to be immoral, but that was about the extent of it. An unusual response (for our respondents) came from this young woman:

> My mother never really communicated anything very negative about homosexuals, but about a friend of hers, she would often say: "What a waste, he was so beautiful!" But my father thinks

---

[14] Goldman, Ari L. "Episcopal Panel Prompts Debate on Gay Couples," *New York Times*, February 1, 1988, p. B3.

[15] Spong, John S. *Living in Sin? A Bishop Rethinks Human Sexuality*, New York: Harper and Row, 1988 (in press).

that homosexuality is a psychological and emotional disorder. I feel very uncomfortable around lesbians but not male homosexuals. One of the girls in my suite in college was a lesbian. She was friendly to me and I was friendly to her, but she didn't try anything with me. I think that the reason why I was so uncomfortable was that if she would hug me like other girls often do, it would mean something different to her.

A female friend of hers told us:

Male homosexuals don't really bother me, but I feel uncomfortable around lesbians. I've lived with male homosexuals in college, but that didn't bother me.

Sometimes behavior that would appear to be homosexual does not have that connotation at all to the participants or members of a particular culture. This was told to us by a young Latino woman raised in the United States:

No, we never heard that it was wrong or sinful for girls to be naked together or to touch each other. As a matter of fact, it was accepted. When I used to go to the Dominican Republic, where many people were poor, even though my family wasn't so poor five girls would have to get into the shower at once because there wasn't that much water. We would be there naked and there was no problem if we touched by accident or we washed each other down, including touching the breasts and genitals. It wasn't only family members but could also include friends and distant relatives as well as servants. But the boys never took showers together, they had to go in alone. I guess there was the fear that boys might have homosexual acts, but no one ever thought that what we girls did to each other was homosexual.

Some homosexual acts seem to be part of the explorations involved in developing sexuality and do not necessarily lead to

178

any adult homosexual preference patterns. For example, this young woman told us:

> One night I was in bed with my female cousin who was older than me. I was about 10 and she was about 12. She put my hand in between her legs and I put her hand in between my legs, and we just played around and thought it felt good. No one caught us or anything, and I didn't think it was a moral *or* an immoral thing to do because no one ever talked about it before.

Such homosexual "play" seems to be fairly common among young boys and girls. Kinsey and his colleagues reported the following on the sexual behavior of males back in 1948 when our society was much more disapproving of homosexuality:

> About half of the older males (48%), and nearer two-thirds (60%) of the boys who were preadolescent at the time they contributed their histories, recall homosexual activity in their preadolescent years. The mean age of the first homosexual contact is about 9 years, 2½ months.[16]

And, for the females:

> Some 6 percent recalled such [homosexual] play by 5 years, and 15 percent by seven years of age. The percentages who had ever had such experience (the accumulative incidence figures) then steadily rose, reaching a level of about 33 percent by the onset of adolescence.[17]

This raises a different kind of moral dilemma related to the definitions of homosexuality. It seems that normal sexual development often involves homosexual as well as heterosexual

---

[16] Kinsey *et al.*, p. 168.
[17] Kinsey, Alfred C., W. Pomeroy, C. Martin and P. Gebhard. *Sexual Behavior in the Human Female*, Philadelphia: W. B. Saunders, 1953, pp. 113–114.

179

sex play among youngsters. If, as so many religious spokes-persons have said, the homosexual *person* is loved by God and accepted by religion but the physical sexual *acts* are condemned, what is our moral standard regarding these homosexual *acts* that are merely part of normal development?

Are parents to pretend that homosexual activities do not exist among preadolescents and avoid mentioning them out of fear that if youngsters know about such activity they might engage in it? Have modern parents come to accept the position that one is born a homosexual, therefore, the homosexual sex play of children is irrelevant? Or do parents avoid the traditional moral teachings concerning homosexuality in order to keep young persons ignorant? This would be a very odd position for anyone who wishes moral standards to be communicated to young people, and yet it appears that this is what is now done. On the other hand, are parents to tell children that they are forbidden to touch each other; should they ban pajama parties because the girls might "get too much pleasure" out of cuddling and holding other girls all night long or might engage in female homosexual activities? Is it reasonably possible to explain to young boys that it is right for young girls to cuddle in bed but not for them? Could there be a legitimate *moral* argument for this position? Maybe that's one reason parents seem to avoid teaching morality to young persons: They are very shaky in their defense of their moral positions regarding the sexual behavior of children. One might even postulate that homophobia (a recent term for fear and/or hatred of homosexuals and homosexuality), is partly the result of parental anxiety, which results from parental awareness of the frequency of homosexual contacts between children.

As we said earlier in this chapter, a homosexual act is not the same as a homosexual preference or identity. If we maintain that it is only the act that is immoral, are parents prepared to interfere with what children do "naturally"? Should we ban children from being alone together and outlaw the slumber party? If children's homosexual acts are not immoral because

180

they are natural expressions of play and affection, how can an adult homosexual act that is the expression of a homosexual nature be immoral?

There seems to be an inconsistency in our attitudes that many people in this society do not recognize. When two women walk hand in hand, no one gives it a thought. When two men do so, they may be physically attacked. When two women dance together, they are just two women dancing together. When two men dance together, do you not assume almost instantly that they are "gay"? When parents see their young daughter hug and kiss another young girl, do they panic as they would if their young son hugged and kissed another boy? As older persons in the homosexual community have told us: Back in the days when homosexuals were arrested, almost never were lesbians similarly arrested. This double standard appears to be not only of recent vintage but, as we said earlier in the chapter, even in the Bible do we find this double standard of condemning male homosexuality while ignoring lesbianism. It is difficult to account for this difference in attitudes then as it is now, without a strong suspicion that because, from biblical days to the present, Judeo-Christian societies have been patriarchial and male dominated, cultural attitudes, mores and laws have usually reflected the male point of view, especially in sexual matters. Thus, the idea of two men having sex with each other may not be to a heterosexual male's liking but the idea of two women having sex with each other may actually turn him on. And so we find that even the most macho, homophobic male will enjoy watching pornographic videos with scenes of two women having sex with each other but would never consider renting a video with two men engaged in homosexual acts. In fact, most of the 1,300 reviews of videos in Robert Rimmer's *The X-Rated Videotape Guide* indicate the presence of at least some lesbian acts in the videos, but virtually no male homosexual acts.[18] While, we acknowledge that our different attitudes

---

[18] Rimmer, Robert H. *The X-Rated Videotape Guide*, New York: Harmony Books, 1986.

181

concerning male-male and female-female body contacts cannot be based solely upon the fact that our societies in the past have been male dominated, we believe that this is certainly one of the factors involved.

Despite a specific Commandment not to commit adultery, do people really get as emotionally upset when they hear of a stranger's adultery as they do when they learn about someone's homosexuality—which is *not* forbidden by any of the Ten Commandments? In sum, has our society become the victim of homophobia rather than righteous about scriptural references?

We realize that there is a great deal of difficulty for most persons when they have to grapple with issues of homosexuality, not only because of religious beliefs but also because of their own understanding or perhaps misunderstanding of the "causes" of homosexuality. They often assume that, as with other issues of sexual morality, one has free will over his or her choices. However, there is no evidence that a homosexual identity and sexual preference is attained by choice. Instead, one is probably born with a homosexual orientation or acquires it within the first few years of life. Can the same principles of moral censure be applied to that which is "natural" for a large segment of the population? Certainly the reasons for homosexuality were no more known in biblical days than today. It seems that the scriptural laws condemning homosexuality presupposed that everyone is a heterosexual and therefore should "act" like a heterosexual. But if it were known then that one's nature cannot change in this area, would homosexuality still have been condemned, and would the homosexual of today still be forced to choose between a life of celibacy or "sinning"? The question is still with us.

CHAPTER 12

A Potpourri
of Thoughts

Many of the feelings, thoughts and perceptions of some of the people we talked with as well as some of our own observations did not fit precisely into any of the previous chapters in the book. Since we feel many of these thoughts have some relevance and importance, we would like to present a few of them here for your thoughtful consideration:

Menstruation

We did not cover menstruation in this book because it really isn't an issue of morality, it is a naturally occurring biological event that cannot be considered either moral or immoral. We do feel, however, that parents often communicate (or for that matter do not communicate) certain attitudes concerning menstruation that have an impact on a young girl's self-image. Such parental messages can also give young boys certain attitudes toward their sisters and other young girls. When a girl has her first menses she is biologically prepared to carry out the greatest creation of God (or nature or the evolutionary process), the creation of human life. This should be a wonderful

183

time in her life—a time to celebrate. In some other cultures, there is a community or tribal party and gifts given to mark this *rite of passage*. In our society, we could have a meaningful "coming of age" party with gifts to the celebrant, who has become a young woman, instead of the vacuous "sweet sixteen" parties that are still given. The time spent in anticipation of this, the years before menarch, could be wisely used not only for sexual information from the parents to the daughter but also for the necessary discussions of the *morality* related to the act and consequences of intercourse.

Out of Sight, Out of Mind

Greater mobility and increased travelling have allowed young people to make friends with persons living in different cities. As a result, sleeping over at the house of a boyfriend's family, or him staying over at her family's house, comes up quite often. This seems to have precipitated an odd but fairly common moral position taken by parents, as described by this young woman:

> My mother knew that I was sleeping with this guy from college because I told her so. But she would never let me sleep with him in my room when he stayed over. He had to stay in the guest room. She knew that he would sneak over to my room, but she would say: "What you do at your house or his house is your business. But when you're at my house, you don't sleep together until you get married." She never caught us together in my room, because my mother has selective blindness. She never said that it wasn't moral, just not right. She never said who said it wasn't right.

We are sure that this mother must have some moral point to make, but we cannot figure out what it is!

Developing Coping Skills

As has been evident throughout this book, when parents attempt to teach morality through fear and repressive prohibitions, a quite unintended and opposite result sometimes occurs. Children learn clever strategies to cope with such meaningless rules and discipline; sometimes it even becomes a game or challenge to outsmart the parents. Think about this young woman's insightful remarks after being asked if it is a good thing for parents to set limits even if they are just prohibitive:

> I think that the one thing about my parents saying: "No, you're not supposed to be doing it," was that I knew that if I got caught, I would be in big trouble. So, I took the precautions not to get caught. Maybe that's a good thing, their telling me not to do it. That clued me in that I needed to be responsible so that I wouldn't get caught.

We hardly think these parents would be pleased if they knew what they had taught their daughter about what it means to be a "responsible" young woman.

AIDS

The fear of AIDS rarely entered into our discussions since the disease knows no moral geography. It is no more a disease of homosexuality than of heterosexuality, no more a disease of nonmarital sex than of marital sex. The fact that rates may be higher in one group or another is a statistical artifact resulting from the manner of transmission. The sexual activity that seems to carry the highest risk for transmission is anal intercourse. But a male who is infected may transmit the disease through unprotected anal intercourse when his partner is another man or a woman. If he is having sex with a woman,

185

he becomes no less likely to infect her with it if she is his loving wife than if she is a casual pick-up.

It seems to us that the moral issues in AIDS are more related to how persons with this disease are mistreated and discriminated against by many segments of society, organized and informal, rather than to any sexual moral issues. Young children who had contracted AIDS through blood transfusions, spouses of narcotics addicts, and spouses of bisexual men have sometimes had to suffer not only from the awareness of their eventual death due to the disease but also to suffer from some insensitive and rejecting communities.

Is the fear of AIDS having any perceptible impact on sexual *behavior*? While many believe that the homosexual community is behaving more responsibly to reduce the possibility of transmission, this is not so apparent in the heterosexual community. On the contrary, the continuing success of singles bars, the list of escort services (often a euphemism for call girl operations) found in the telephone business pages and the numerous ads for prostitutes in various papers would seem to indicate little change in this direction.

Only one of our respondents, a young woman, made any reference to changing sexual lifestyles. She told us that her mother was basically opposed to her having premarital sex because it might lead to many sex partners, but she was less opposed to her living with a young man whom she might later marry. The mother's reasoning was that her daughter would be safe from AIDS if she were living with a man because she would have only one partner. This is an interesting consideration and one we are sure will be entertained by more and more parents unless we learn to control this disease.

About the Lay People We Interviewed

We have avoided presenting any statistics about the characteristics of the sample we used for this book because we did not want to give the impression that we chose people in a systematically random manner or that the sample we used was statistically representative of the country as a whole. This was not that kind of study. If someone wishes to develop a quantitative study to measure the precise degree to which sexual morality is or is not taught, we would be happy to assist them, but this is not necessary for us. It is not from a lack of knowledge concerning the methodology of social science—Lou Lieberman has taught undergraduate and graduate research methods courses for many years. We were not out to prove anything but to make you think about something we care about very strongly.

The people we talked with came from all walks of life and from a wide variety of ages, races, religions and levels of sophistication. We have chosen to present quotations from mostly younger persons because they are now or soon will be faced with the joys and heartaches of raising young children themselves. Most were very intelligent and verbal regardless of their educational level, although many were going to college or had graduated. For the most part, they were nice people, the kind you would like to have for friends and neighbors. They were kind and caring people—concerned about their fellow humans, about how children should be raised and about the values that most of us would agree with.

Most of our respondents were what we would consider to be religious and were regular churchgoers (is there such a phrase as "regular synagoguegoer?"). With few exceptions, most had a consistent religious upbringing and training. One thing struck and impressed us: Despite the frequency and extent to which they violated their religion's moral norms, *they all felt that they were moral and good people*. They were concerned about moral issues—not only sexual moral issues but also issues of war and poverty, exploitation and discrimination and many other issues. In the sexual areas, we sensed they felt they had been let down and ignored by their religion, which had been afraid to come to grips with sexual moral issues and conflicts. There was

187

virtually no sex education in the backgrounds of our respondents, except from whatever they learned from their peers and an occasional human sexuality course in high school or college, which usually did not go into morals or values.

Rarely did anyone present a moral basis for their sexual codes of conduct. More often than not, they seemed uncomfortable with discussions of morality *per se*, but would consider "not hurting anyone" as the *sine qua non* of their moral beliefs. For the most part, religion seemed to be compartmentalized from their beliefs about sexual conduct. Most expressed the view that they would teach their children to be moral, but in an individualized manner rather than teaching a traditional religious view. This was true even for those with strong religious ties.

Nearly all admitted confronting their emerging sexuality with great apprehension, and using the trial and error method of developing sexual maturity—and acknowledging many mistakes in the absence of guidance. Consequently, their emerging sexual self-image was not derived from well-considered choices but rather from the results of impulsive actions that often had painful outcomes.

CHAPTER 13

Conclusion and Recommendations

We are sure that some people are wondering exactly where we stand on the different moral issues we have discussed in this book. As we said at the outset, our task has been to raise consciousness about the necessity to make people "morally literate"; it is not for us to judge what is or is not moral for others in any given situation. The differences in moral beliefs within religions, the questioning of traditional positions by theologians, the different religious and ethical communities within the United States and the rest of Western culture make it impossible for any individual to espouse moral guidelines that will be applicable to everyone. What we have tried to convey is the necessity for all persons to have a moral position and set of guidelines to help them make the appropriate sexual choices they face throughout their lives, as children as well as adults. What the specific moral code and position may be is not as important as the early and continuing education in moral and ethical values.

Our research and interviews with both lay persons and professionals revealed a startling parallel: Whereas previous generations did not openly discuss sexuality, current generations do not discuss morality. Thus, the means for learning

189

sexual morality today is very similar to what the means for learning about sexual behavior used to be. (But one difference is that people once hungered for sexual knowledge—but who craves moral knowledge today?) When the youth of earlier generations were growing up, it was generally accepted that they learned about sex on a catch-as-catch-can basis. That is, they learned what sex was all about by looking up forbidden words in the dictionary, trying to sneak an "adults only" book out of the library, comparing notes with friends on sex play (bragging or concealing as the case may be), looking at the pornographic "2 by 4s" that were passed on from kid to kid for a price; buying a much coveted "French postcard", playing "you show me yours and I'll show you mine" and other innocent and not so innocent games, and obtaining dubious "reference" books on sex. The scene of the sensitive parents sitting down with their children and teaching them in wise and delicate terms about "the birds and the bees" was virtually unknown to most. Such wise counseling may have taken place among the more educated and elite in this country and in Europe, but it seems most youngsters learned about sex the hard way, from the "street"—for many, this turned out to be a disastrous way. Sex education was not only unknown but even public discussions of sex were all but forbidden. Today it is different. There is a wealth of good, reliable sources of information about human sexuality for people of all ages and classes. Some may argue that the abundance of this easily available information is not a good thing, but no one can deny that it exists.

Although both the young and old currently have fairly easy access to the "facts of life," there is still a void when it comes to the morality surrounding these facts. Unfortunately, young and old today don't seem as eager to learn about morality as previous generations were to learn about sex. As open as we are today in the discussion of sexual matters, we appear to be as silent about sexual morality as we once were about "the birds and the bees." We now teach sexual literacy, but we appear unable, too embarrassed, confused and even frightened to discuss sexual morality. With few exceptions, primarily in those religions that are very demanding of worshippers' commitment and involvement in all aspects of religious life, our churches, synagogues and temples do not appear to teach sexual morality to their congregants and members, be they adults or children. Similarly, parents do not teach sexual morality to their children, although some teach prohibition and fear and think that it is morality. Most parents do not know the moral bases for judging the correctness of sexual expressions from the perspective of their own religion. And, as we have learned from public school administrators: Heaven forbid that the public schools should mention *morality* in the teaching of sex education—it would probably violate fourteen subsections of twenty-three different codes. Who then is teaching our sexual moral standards? In general, no one! It is ironic, paradoxical and in some fashion bizarre that we have opened doors to the free exchange of information on sexual behavior, techniques, dysfunctions and pleasure but have hidden morality in the closet as if there were fear it was contained in a Pandora's box.

As we said at the beginning of this book, the glib politicians and religious leaders who urge us to return to traditional morality in the area of sexual behavior may not realize, if they are honest, that they are confusing moral behavior with re- pressive behavior. We wonder if they know any more about morality than the people whom they condemn, or whether they have created a mythical morality out of wishful thinking. Every religious and humanistic system of behavior has a moral base with a certain logic pointing to ethical values and behaviors in the sexual area. Many of these moral systems are similar— all must be taught and learned for them to have meaning for an individual. At the same time, many adherents of these moral systems are undergoing examinations of the legitimacy and relevancy of their moral codes. How can average people be expected to make wise choices in sexual behavior when they have not been taught the traditional beliefs as well as the contemplations of changes in these beliefs? Making correct

191

choices implies knowledge of alternatives. Unfortunately, moral illiteracy appears to be the norm, even among those people who consider themselves strong religious adherents. We know that this will be a highly controversial statement and we are already imagining all the people who will say: "Not us, it must be the other family (or religion)." We were struck with the very frank and revealing observation and insight on this topic told to us by the Evangelist minister Dr. Robert H. Schuller from the Crystal Cathedral in California:

> Whether or not there has been a decline in sexual morality in particular is not clear because we don't know what was happening even two or three generations ago. However, I do have the perception that in Western civilization, from its Greco-Roman influences through the Renaissance, there has been a long standing tendency *not* to develop persons as moral creatures, in my opinion. We have not given human beings the teaching that they should be leaders—and a leader is a person who is aware of his personhood, meaning his freedom to make choices. But basically, the dominant influence of Christianity, that is, Roman Catholicism and Protestantism, resulted in a tendency which was not to train believers to be persons or leaders or individual thinkers—hence truly moral creatures—but rather to be follow-ers. The church would make the decisions as to what ought to be done, and the believers would be expected to learn what ought to be done, and then they were supposed to obey.
>
> If that has been a dominant strain in character development in Western civilization, then I would have to say that we have a deep-seated conflict of morality [between being followers and being individual thinkers] going all the way back. It is much deeper than just the sexual aspect, but it definitely will impact on the sexual aspect. That means that when we look at society today, we find that people, for the most part, were never taught to be moral creatures, they were taught to be followers. At one time, they recognized the church as the decision-making force and followed the herd. The head of the herd may be a pope, the head of the herd may be a Protestant pastor, the head of

the herd may be a rabbi, the head of the herd may be a Dr. Schuller. If that is the kind of person that religions produce, then we can expect that when religion loses some of its impact, as in modern pluralistic society, people become more likely to follow the social herd. They may think that they are more free by not following the religious herd, but they are just as unaware that they are not free to choose among options and are still just following another herd.

On the whole, we are in agreement with this strong statement by Dr. Schuller. A history of religious warfare and persecution, of political hatreds resulting in war, of large numbers of humans being cruel to other humans can only underscore that morality must be an active pursuit and that when it is merely passive, it can result in great danger to society. Even sexual morality is not merely an individual concern since the consequences of inappropriate sexual choices can impact on society in the many ways we have discussed. A recent article in the *New York Times Magazine* illustrates how moral decision making and moral responsibility have become so irrelevant for many. After inter-viewing a number of very "eligible" bachelors, the author borders on applauding the lifestyle of these men, including their sexual involvements without commitment:

To judge from my interviews, however, not to mention my memory, bachelorhood is not the last refuge of the male scoundrel. Nor is it just a dodge for men obsessed with careers or "spoiled" by the easy availability of premarital sex. I was impressed by the men I talked with, their candor and intro-spection, and I came away thinking bachelorhood a viable choice. Talking to single men, in fact, I felt a tinge of envy and nostalgia. My encounters pulled me vividly back to the time when giving up my bachelorhood had seemed a great sacrifice.

I enjoyed being single, enjoyed the excitement of seeing someone new, every mundane detail about her exotic. At dinner or at a party there was the thrilling realization that an attraction was mutual. It could be like a drug, being single and dating, with its rush of sudden intimacy with a stranger.[1]

While the author does go on to say that for many bachelors in their 30s and 40s the reality is not so idyllic, unfortunately, he does not take the time to mention a few words about the moral and modelling implications of this behavior. If sex outside of marriage is in no way a moral issue for some of our best and our brightest young men, this too, by its very omission, is a moral message: It is O.K. for these men to have sex outside of marriage. But if it is O.K. for them in their 30s, why not for those in their 20s? And if it is O.K. for those in their 20s, why not their teens? Privilege based on age is a form of age discrimination against those who are not in the privileged age category. We are sure that many might argue that these men are more "mature" or "responsible," but we also know that age does not guarantee either quality in a person. There are many teenagers we know who appear to be more responsible than many adults. We are not suggesting that 40-year-olds should behave as 14-year-olds or vice versa but rather that both need to be guided by moral standards. The 40-year-old and the 14-year-old should both understand the difference between a moral and an ego-centered choice in sexual behavior. If our society has failed by making morality irrelevant to both, the problem is with the institutions out of which moral precepts are developed and transmitted, not with people who have been given few if any moral standards with which to work.

Some people may accuse us of popularizing such esoteric concepts as morality and ethics. To these critics we say: "Yes, indeed!" That's what we need to do—we need to bring the discussion of morality to the place where it belongs, into the lives of the masses of people, instead of leaving it to the abstruse

---

[1]Green, Theophilius. "Why Wed? The Ambivalent American Bachelor." *New York Times Magazine*, November 15, 1987, p. 24.

hairsplitting of theologians and scholars. We do not mean to imply that we don't need theologians and scholars. We need them, but they must learn to convert their obscure rhetoric to plain language so that *all of us* can understand morality and teach it to our developing children, rather than the destructive authoritarianism that so many have relied upon. Without this, the social problems resulting from poor sexual choices will not be ameliorated.

This issue, therefore, raises a fundamental problem that we have repeatedly touched upon: Sexual values based upon a consistent and well thought out system of ethics and morality is almost totally out of the minds of many people of all ages when they have to make choices in the area of sexual behavior. We repeat again, prohibition based on fear is not morality. If all we can instill in young people is fear of the consequences of sexual activity: fear of disease, fear of pregnancy, fear of exposure, fear of father's punishment, and even fear of God's punishment, then when people no longer fear that they may get caught they might act in whatever manner they please. In these circumstances, the spontaneity and the passion of the moment, in the absence of built-in brakes to help someone avoid making the wrong choices, could lead to unwanted consequences. Fear of apprehension and punishment is not the most effective way of ensuring nondestructive behavior. As proof, all we have to do is to look at the failure of our past policy of increasing criminal penalties for drug use as the means of preventing people from using the illicit drugs. We believe that most people would not steal, even if they knew they wouldn't be caught, not because of fear but because of a conscience that whispers to them that it is wrong.

The failure of our religious institutions to convey meaningful moral standards to their followers was clear from our respondents. Many people who wanted closer ties and spiritual guidance instead of authoritarianism from their religion felt they were being shut out. From a young woman:

195

Am I a good Catholic? It depends. To me a Catholic is someone who goes to church every Sunday. That is what we were taught. I don't agree with that. As far as I'm concerned, if I believe in God and love and do good, I'm a good Catholic. But we were taught to go to church every Sunday and to support the church financially and in other ways. Even though I don't do that, I still feel I'm a good person, I don't do any harm to anybody, I don't kill anybody. So that's a good Catholic to me. I don't feel that I have to obey these rules written down by priests. Who knows where these rules, these laws, come from.

The ambiguity as well as the yearning for moral and ethical teaching that so many people indicated to us came even from people who had maximum exposure to religious teaching in parochial schools. When we asked one young man whether he thought the parochial schools like the one he had attended do a good job of teaching morals and values, he replied at length:

Yes, I think they do. Because even though you may wind up going through the whole thing of rejecting your religion, you still will be taught, and have drummed into you, certain codes of conduct, moral codes. Basically, these come from the Ten Commandments. In the Catholic schools, they do try to teach you what is right and wrong in the religion classes. They sometimes paint it as if it were God's word, but even if you reject the religion, you still wind up having the basic values left behind, like it's not right to covet your neighbor's wife, it's not right to steal, it's wrong to commit murder, and so forth.

. . . when we have children, we might not send them to Catholic schools. . . . [U]nless we can get them into good public schools, I would prefer they go to a Catholic or some other religious school where they can get some training in morals as well as reading and arithmetic. . . . I would have no objection to sending my child to an Episcopal school because I'm more concerned in giving the kid a good solid education, of not just the basic fundamentals but also some moral values which you will not get in public schools and which you may get in a distorted way in Catholic schools.

196

I think that the feeling many of the kids in my parochial school had was that everybody is passing the buck. The nuns and brothers could tell us the church's position on oral sex and so forth, but they really couldn't discuss it with us. They assumed the family would discuss these things and it got them off the hook. [The family says:] "Learn it from the church." It's going to create a lot of confusion in sexual mores, I think, because kids are going to get caught in this battle between the church and the family and society. They're going to have to sit back and try and figure out for themselves what's right and what's wrong. Now I think I was able to figure out on my own, fairly decently, what's right and what's wrong. But a lot of other kids may not be able to and that's where there is going to be a lot of problems and a lot of confusion because of all this kicking back and forth of the issue: Who is responsible for sex education, and who is responsible for teaching the moral and religious aspects of it and the teaching of values. No one ever taught me [how to make a right decision based on a moral choice for new situations] until I took theology courses in a catholic university. I got a little bit about what things to take into account: the effect that your decision is going to have on you; the effect that your decision is going to have on others; what is the right thing to do; who is going to benefit and how. But the bottom line is that we were told that basically you are the one who has to make the choice.

As we noted in several chapters, the ethical principle by which parents communicate morality to their children seems to be the acceptance of community standards for what is right or wrong, acceptable or unacceptable. They judge morality on the basis of "What will the neighbors say?" or by using the behavior of a neighbor's child as an example of "good" or "bad" moral behavior. Given this, it should come as no surprise to parents when their teenage children deviate from the rules of conduct they are taught because they too are using the standards of their community—their community of peers. They no more want to stand out from their peers by following

197

different values and behavior than the parents of a teenage daughter want her protruding belly to be a visible indication of her unacceptable behavior in the parents' community. Children want to conform as much as parents do—but they do not, and cannot, follow the same community norms. Youngsters are living in a different generation and frequently in a different community. Conformity as a means of social control is a two-edged sword. Standards are needed, but they should be based on positive, understandable principles, not on what the neighbors are doing. This is reflected in another excellent observation by Dr. Schuller:

> There is a need to teach moral principles to our youth, particularly in a pluralistic society where boundaries seem to be removed. I happen to believe that a person who is without boundaries is setting himself up for other psychological problems. When boundaries are removed, people seem to get very insecure because there is a confusion of expectations. They seem to say: "Let me know if I am right or wrong—I can live with the rules, but please let me know what the rules are."
>
> These rules of right and wrong should be taught, but they should be taught positively and not negatively. When you do it positively, you say to people: "I have what I think might bring you greater happiness."

O.K. By now you are in complete agreement with us and are raring to go take morality out of the closet and to make morality, especially sexual morality, as interesting to talk about and study as "How to make your partner sexually satisfied." What we can do?

First, and least controversial, let our religious leaders do a little "soul searching." (Pardon the pun.) Is morality, including sexual morality, being taught in a meaningful and useful way to *all* members of the congregation? Are their parishioners morally literate? What is the curriculum in parochial schools and Sunday schools and afternoon schools regarding morality?

Do the religious leaders even know? We bet they do not! The institution of religion has historically had the responsibility for the elaboration and interpretations not only of moral implications and law in scripture but also of the complex task of fitting historical tradition into changing societies. At no time in history have societies changed more rapidly than in recent decades. It is the responsibility of the religious institutions to educate and provide us with guidelines for morality, and specifically in the area in which religion has become so fuzzy: sexual morality.

Second, if parents are to have the primary responsibility for the *transmission* of moral norms, as we believe they should, then they have a right to be educated in this very important parental task. If some parents don't wish to exercise this responsibility to get the knowledge and to teach it to their children, then please, dear parents, be so wise as to turn this moral education over to someone else. You have no right to leave children stripped of morality but fearful of punishment. Parents have an obligation to society to help their children learn to be good members of society. Without a good moral base, they will often grope their way into the wrong choices. Go to your churches and synagogues and demand classes in sexual morality and moral literacy.

Third, we say to parents, ministers, rabbis, priests, the moral right, the moral left and the moral in-between: Don't be afraid of sex education. Sexual morality without sexual education is an abstraction that tends to confuse people, particularly young people. If we cannot talk about sexual behavior, how can we talk about sexual morality? If we perpetuate false myths about sexual behavior, our children, who usually know better, will believe that our sexual morality is also no more than false myths. Honesty in one requires honesty in the other. If a person is too embarrassed to talk or incapable of talking about sexual behavior, we believe that person is probably also too embarrassed to talk or incapable of talking about sexual morality. We must realize and remember that both sex education and moral education must be appropriately geared to age and

199

prior knowledge. One cannot say: "Don't commit adultery," to a young person who does not know what adultery means, and one cannot know what adultery means without knowing what kinds of sexual behaviors take place between men and women.

Fourth, our churches and synagogues need more peer leadership in moral literacy. Unfortuately, too many young persons feel uncomfortable when they talk about sexual morality with adults. Sometimes it seems that young people always think that their generation discovered sex and that their parents lost interest in the subject two weeks after the last child was conceived. But when they discuss sexual issues with each other, it seems they rarely discuss the moral issues. It's not that they can't discuss them, they just rarely come up. We think that it would be a good idea for the different religions to reach out more through young people to bring the moral teachings to their peers *and* to their parents. We suspect that young people would get a kick out of teaching morality to a group of their elders. We are sure they would do a better job than their elders did to them.

Our **fifth** suggestion is the most controversial and also the most necessary to implement. Many people will say that our first four suggestions are all fine and good but would argue that the young people who are already involved in their churches and synagogues are not the ones who are likely to get into trouble through incorrect choices. For the most part we would agree. However, are we just to throw up our hands concerning the vast numbers of people of all ages who are not affiliated with and do not go to religious schools and institutions? Who is to train them in moral decision making? We believe that there is only one institution that has this capability: the public school system.

We are quite aware of the history of the struggle for separation of church and state in this country, and we support the separation as much as anyone. But we do not believe that the *study* of morality, even of its relationship to religion, is the same as the promulgation of religion. We know that a fine line separates the two, and safeguards will have to be built in order to ensure that the line is not crossed. But the issue of morality is not merely one of religion; there are secular moralities and value systems just as there are religious ones. Atheists need moral guidelines just as devout religious believers do. And who is to say that believers are more likely to be moral than atheists? Everyone can profit from the study of comparative morality. We believe that this will not weaken one's faith but actually strengthen it because it is in the thinking and examining and questioning that one's faith matures, not in the passive acceptance of "the truth." Public schools can serve as an ideal forum for learning about and exploring a variety of moral perspectives so that youngsters can establish a firm moral base, we hope in line with their traditional background, and, at the same time, can appreciate and be tolerant of alternative views that others may hold. However, we are not trying to give the impression that parents should abrogate their responsibility for moral training in favor of the schools. We believe that this still should be part of the parenting roles. But, for those cases where parents do not do this, somebody must. Even for those children where there is some moral training at home or in a religious setting, receiving the reinforcement of parallel moral training and relating to these issues with their *peers*, in the secular setting of a public school, can be a very enriching experience.

Who will teach this in the schools? What will the content be? How do we avoid problems of church/state issues? How do we avoid religious divisiveness? We can't answer these questions or many others like them that may easily be raised because the process of developing answers to these questions cannot begin until there is the collective will of leaders in the churches, schools, and community that this is a necessary undertaking. Certainly, whatever good can come out of this will only result from a combination of efforts of schools, churches, parents, *and* children.

Sixth and finally, what can the two of us do to move all this along? The typical academic or governmental response we have heard so often is: When in doubt, do a study. We will do more than a study, we will develop a *Center for the Study of Sexual Ethics*, perhaps at John Jay College of the City University of New York or at New York University—two universities where we are affiliated, but certainly in an academic and urban setting. We are very encouraged by the response to our plans from scholars, teachers, ministers, physicians and many others concerned with the same issues we have presented in this book.

The main objective of this center will be for it to become a forum for all parts of the community concerned with sexual morality and ethics: religions, medicine, pharmaceutical companies, the criminal justice system, advertising, education, parents and children. As indicated by this list, the center will take a broad perspective on sexual ethics to include not only immediate questions of sexual behavior but also issues of sexual harassment, treatment of sexual offenders, the teaching of values in sex education curricula, sex crimes, mass media influences on sexual ethics, etc. The center will conduct conferences, encourage research, develop curricula, and publish materials, with special emphasis on bridging the gulf between the religious and secular communities in the area of sexual morality.

It is not the intent of this center to formulate or profess one point of view or to be a forum for those with the proverbial "ax to grind." Our only firm and consistent orientation will be: *Appropriate sexual choices require education, knowledge and moral as well as ethical considerations.*

Can we accomplish each of the six objectives listed above? We doubt it, but as we said near the beginning of the book: "It is not thy duty to complete the work, but neither art thou free to desist from it." (*The Talmud, Ethics of the Fathers*, II, Mishna 16).

Index

Nipple, 159
Noah, 62, 98
Nonmarital sex, 28, 166, 167,
  185
Nontraditional unions, 177
Normlessness, 29, 105
Norms, 11, 52, 57
Norton, Eleanor Holmes, 136
Nudity, 42, 48, 49, 50, 166
  nudist beaches, 58, 69
  nudist camps, 57, 58, 60, 61,
    63
  social nudism, 58
  social nudist, 59
Nuns, 47, 124, 154, 197

Oedipal, 65
Onan, 34, 42, 43
  Onanism, 36, 37, 130
Open marraige, 116, 122
Oral contraceptive, 80, 134
Oral sex, 43, 85, 92, 197
Orgasm, 23, 41, 50, 117, 157
  orgasm, childhood, 31

P'ru ur'vu, 139
Pagan, 63, 174
Pain, 49, 50
Pajama parties, 180
Parents, 8, 9, 18, 21, 26, 31, 43,
  44, 45, 49, 53, 101, 106,
  109, 199, 200, 201, 202
  parental avoidance, 44
  parental denial, 44
  parental modelling, 125
Parochial schools, 42, 47, 55, 70,
  93, 97, 141, 152, 162, 196,
  199

Patai, Dr. Raphael, 146, 147,
  172, 173
Paternity, 129
Paul, St., 105, 153, 174
Pediatrician, 51
Peers, 20, 198
  peer influence, 127
  peer leadership, 200
Penance, 36
Penis, 35, 37, 48, 50, 62–64,
  132, 158, 159
Permissiveness
  with affection, 87, 90
  without affection, 86, 89, 91
Perversion, 158
Pessary cap, 80
Pharmaceutical companies, 202
Philosophers, 146, 147
Physicians, 59, 61, 149, 202
Piaget, Dr. Jean, 52
Pimples, 36
Plato, 146, 172
Playboy, 113
Plymouth, 78
Police, 124, 152
Political, 20
Politicians, 18, 191
Pompadour, Madame de, 115
Pope Pius IX, 149
Pope Pius XI, 81
Pope Sixtus V, 149
Pornographic videos, 181
Postmarital sex, 75
Poverty, 135
Preadolescent, 51, 179
Pregnancy, 16, 28, 78, 88, 91,
  100, 110, 130, 133, 136,
  142, 148, 149, 151, 152,
  195

Index

Premarital sex, 27, 75, 86, 87
Prepubescent, 52, 55
Presbyterians, 115
Preteens, 43, 44, 54, 55
Priests, 38, 45, 48, 87, 124, 138,
    154, 196, 199
Pro-choice, 151
Procreation, 28, 35, 39, 47, 55
Prohibition, 60, 68, 72, 184, 195
Prostitutes, 84, 186
Protestantism, 27–29, 40, 98,
    103, 108, 115, 162, 192
Psychiatrists, 171
Psychological tensions, 127
Psychologists, 36, 51, 57, 171
Psychopathic, 37
Psychosexual development, 55
Psychotherapists, 49, 51
Puberty, 43, 52, 76
Public schools, 120, 190, 200,
    201
Pudenda, 63
Puerto Rican, 164
Puerto Rico, 71, 125, 142, 153
Puritans, 115

Quakers, 115
Quickening, 148, 156

Rabbis, 27, 43, 87, 152, 193, 199
Race, 44
Rape, 16, 115, 160, 174
Regulations, 20, 35
Reiss, Dr. Ira L., 79, 86, 89, 90
Released-time, 120
Religion, 6, 14, 24, 25, 26, 27,
    35, 38, 44, 49, 52, 62, 85,
    101, 124, 129, 137, 140,
    202

Religious leaders, 18, 38, 167,
    191, 199
Religious educators, 49
Religious schools, 200
Renaissance, 192
Rhode Island, 78
Rhythm method, 139
Rimmer, Robert, 181
Rite of passage, 184
Robin Hood, 24
Roe v. *Wade*, 151
Roman Catholic, 28, 35, 38, 64,
    84, 85, 97, 102, 104, 123,
    131, 139, 140, 149, 152,
    154, 161, 195
  Catholicism, 28, 103, 108,
    124, 150, 192
  church, 27, 77, 84, 98, 140
  school, 42, 54, 196
  university, 197
Roman culture, 172
Romans, 146, 174
Rome, 63, 114
Rousseau, Jean-Jacques, 36
Rules, 25

Sacraments, 126
Saint and satyr complex, 94
Sanskrit, 159
Saul, 62
Scholars, 194, 202
Schools, 20, 40, 101, 110, 201
Schuller, Dr. Robert E., 175,
    191, 192, 193, 198
Scripture, 177, 182, 199
Second Vatican Council, 28, 39,
    84, 85, 102, 103
Secular moralities, 201
Secularism, 25

210